Henry Cordonnier

My Gospel

BookSurge   Charleston

Imprimatur: Reverend Joseph R. Binzer
           Vicar General
           Archdiocese of Cincinnati
           Cincinnati, Ohio
           December 20, 2007

The Nihil Obstat and the Imprimatur are official declarations that a book or pamphlet is free from doctrinal or moral error. No implication is contained therein that those who granted the Nihil Obstat or Imprimatur agree with the contents or statements expressed.

Cover Design by Nikki Day
Eucharist Photo provided by Life Teen © 2008

Orders (937) 295-2626
www.mygospelbook.com

Dedicated to my beloved wife Ann

*"Charm is deceptive and beauty fleeting, but the woman
who fears the Lord is to be praised."*
Proverbs 31:30

Acknowledgements

I want to thank my teaching colleague Matt Cordonnier for his constant encouragement to write this book. I also want to thank Fr. Christopher Armstrong for his many helpful comments and his friendship. Many thanks to Jess Sargent, Maddie Goodwin, Maggie Cordonnier, and Kiefer King for typing the manuscript. I am also very grateful to Kevin Cameron for all his technical help in formatting this book and creating the website. Also, I want to thank Nikki Day for her beautiful cover design.

Finally, many of the names in the book have been changed to protect the privacy of those persons.

Table of Contents

Preface

A frozen steak from the freezer and a hot, juicy steak from the grill are both steak, but the one which has been over the fire is much more appealing to me.

A mediocre Catholic going through some of the motions of religion and a Spirit-filled Catholic burning with the love of God are both Catholics, but the one on fire is much more appealing to me and to a world that desperately needs to know the love of Jesus.

This book has been written with those "slightly chilled" Catholics in mind - Catholics who may have spent years in CCD classes or in Catholic schools or sitting through Sunday Masses and have mostly experienced boredom. It has been written with the hope that it will serve as a spark that will ignite a fire of love for God in their hearts. If this book can help someone to realize the depth of Jesus' love for them along with the beauty and power of the Catholic Faith, then it will have served its purpose.

I was an unhappy, frost-bitten Catholic who went through the motions of religion for years but never really knew the love and power of Jesus that was right in front of me. Through the mercy of God my eyes were opened, and I was able to see Jesus and experience His love which has transformed my life.

Everything that I could possibly desire I found in the Catholic Church. I have found the pearl of great price, and I want to share my joy with you. I hope that reading about some of my experiences will help you to discover the greatest treasure in the world, Jesus and His Church.

Introduction

It's Heaven all the way to Heaven, and it's Hell all the way to Hell. This describes my life and in fact, everyone's life. Let me explain.

When I entered into a relationship with Jesus as my Lord and Savior, I found the true love of my life; an unconditional love that was a transforming power unlike anything else in the world. Living with Jesus became Heaven on earth.

Of course, truly following Jesus entails many hardships. The wisdom of this world says that you can't be happy in the midst of trial and tribulation, but this world is wrong. Living with Jesus makes all the difference in the world. The same circumstances that would be a crushing burden for others can actually be a joyful experience for the person who is in love with Jesus. Martyrs have actually gone to their deaths with smiles on their faces. How is that possible? It's possible because they are in union with Jesus.

Jesus said, "*My yoke is sweet, my burden is light.*"

A yoke is a piece of wood that fits over the neck of two oxen and binds them together. It enables them to pull the load together. The yoke of Jesus is sweet because it binds you to Jesus. What could be better or sweeter than to be joined to the most loving and powerful person in the world? When you live your life walking in union with Jesus, it is really Heaven on earth because you're with Jesus, *the one you love*. The burden is light and easy to pull even if the weight is tremendous because the power to pull it comes, not from you, but from Almighty God who is pulling alongside of you. It's truly

Heaven all the way to Heaven as you work, live, and walk in union with the one you love and who loves you perfectly.

But what if you're pulling the plow alone or your life is "yoked" to sin and evil? Then each day is a terrible struggle and a painful experience. It's a living Hell as you walk each day without the power and love of Jesus beside you. Just look at the world around you. So many people living desperate, hopeless lives filled with so much pain due to sinful addictions, broken families and relationships, and one terrible decision after the next. By age twenty many people's lives are no more than scrambled eggs. Many don't even make it to twenty.

A life without Jesus is a hell of a life. Our sins drag us down and each day the burden becomes more unbearable. A life without Jesus gets worse and worse until one day that life comes to an end and then that poor soul faces an eternity without Jesus. That's exactly what Hell is, never knowing the sweet love of Jesus, or anyone else, for all eternity. *To be stuck without love forever.* It makes me tremble just to think of it. It is terrible beyond words.

My dear Friend, I'm writing this book so that you might believe in Jesus and find happiness both here on this earth and in Heaven forever. As you read about the wonderful things that Jesus has done in my life, I want you to know that He will do the same for you. Jesus loves you so much that He would have died on the cross to save only you. Right now you might find that hard to believe, as I once did, but read this book and open your heart to Him and you too will find the Way, the Truth, and the Life.

Part I
Conversion

Dad and Mom

I was born in 1953, the son of Norbert and Margaret Cordonnier. There were seven older brothers in the family, and we lived on a dairy farm in west central Ohio. My parents were very good Catholics who saw their faith as the center of their lives. My mother had spent two years in the convent but decided that the religious life was not her vocation. Dad was a solid Catholic who obeyed the laws of the Church and went on some men's retreats over the years.

Our family life had a Catholic flavor that was unmistakable. We prayed the rosary on our knees every evening as a family in the living room. There was religious art in every room of our house. Mom would remind us every morning to say our prayers and offer our day to God. We had religion classes at school and those lessons were reinforced at home. It seemed like we were always going to church and we had to be there early and stay late.

The Wrong Path

When I made my First Communion at age seven, I felt close to God but that closeness began to slip away during the junior high years. It was in the mid 1960's when the whole nation seemed to be losing its mind over sex, drugs, and rock and roll, and my life was going the same direction. I never experimented with drugs because my drug of choice was alcohol. In my small Midwest town, alcohol was king and there weren't a lot of other drugs around at that time, so I began to drink in high school. I was getting drunk once or twice weekly. In the rural area where I lived it was quite common for teenagers to get drunk. Liquor laws were seldom enforced, and the local bars were only too happy to sell booze to minors. I had a girlfriend whose dad owned and operated a local bar, and during my sophomore year I spent a lot of nights getting wasted there. I had to be very sneaky to get away with this bad behavior because if my parents had found out they would have been very upset. After all, they were really good and holy people who had never given me a bad example and who had always taught me the right way to live. Now I was committing sins that went against all my religious training, and I didn't want to get caught. So I resorted to all kinds of lying and deception in order to get away with my drinking binges. This pattern of be-havior continued throughout my junior and senior year of high school until I graduated in 1971. During this time my conscience was always convicting me of my sinful-ness. I went to confession a lot and never missed Sunday Mass because these sacraments were a regular part of my family's life. Even though God's grace was always there, I continued down the wrong path.

I arrived at Miami University in Oxford, Ohio, in the fall of 1971. Roger was my best friend growing up and he and I would be roommates for the next four years at college. Away from all the work on my dad's dairy farm, I felt like college was a vacation so I lived it up. My sinful habits only grew worse. In addition to my drunkenness, sexual impurity, and cursing, I added laziness and complete self-centeredness. This life might sound pretty sinful, but actually it was pretty routine stuff for most of the guys who lived in my fraternity. In fact, many of my fraternity brothers were living even worse lives than me. But very few of them had the inner spiritual turmoil that I suffered. I had been raised in such a good Catholic environment and my conscience wouldn't let me forget it. While most everyone at college had given up on God and going to church, I went to Confession and Mass every Saturday evening to fulfill my Sunday obligation. If I didn't get there in time for Confession then I wouldn't be able to go to Holy Communion because I was living in mortal sin and to go to Holy Communion would have been another mortal sin of sacrilege. There was a spiritual war going on inside of me. I knew what was right and I wanted to do it, but I seemed powerless to stop myself from sins that had become strong habits through years of practice. Looking back on those days, I can understand the words of St. Paul, "*I do not do what I want to do, but what I hate... what a wretched man I am!*"

My life during the four years at Miami University was very routine. It was an endless cycle of beer blasts and partying with some classes in between. I never thought of myself as an alcoholic at the time, but I surely must have been. By the time I was a senior I started each day by getting out of bed about noon and pouring myself a twelve ounce glass full of straight whiskey over a couple of ice cubes. That was breakfast. Even though I drank everyday I was still a "B" average student and on schedule to graduate early.

I can only thank God that he spared me from serious injury or death due to my drunkenness. I often drove drunk and on two occasions fell from a moving vehicle into the ditch. One night I drank twelve bottles of wine and had to spend three days in the hospital recuperating. In my opinion, it was the prayers of my saintly parents that called down God's mercy upon me and spared my life. Even though I was away at college and they didn't know about my sinful lifestyle, they were in the habit of interceding for all of their children daily, and I believe their prayers protected me.

I would go to confession face-to-face and the priest knew me very well. One day he said, "Henry, you're living a hell of a life!" I hung my head and replied, "I know, but I don't know how to stop."

He said, "You have one thing in your favor, at least you keep coming back to confession. Don't give up."

Well, I didn't give up but I really had no idea how I was ever going to break out of my sinful habits that had enslaved me for the previous eight years. I just continued to travel down the road of life without a map or a plan. But God had a plan for me. My life was about to change.

A New Direction

I went home for Thanksgiving during my senior year. At home my Dad privately informed me that something wonderful had happened to him. He had been on a Catholic retreat and while there he had opened his heart to the Holy Spirit in a new way. He said that he had experienced the "Baptism in the Holy Spirit" and had received the gift of tongues. He demonstrated this gift by speaking in a foreign language that he had never learned. He urged me to open myself up to God. Everything that my Dad described to me seemed very strange. I had never heard of anyone speaking in tongues in modern times, and I really didn't know what to make of it. Dad seemed very happy and I thought it was fine for him, but it really didn't have anything to do with me. I went back to college and life went on as before.

About three months later I met Kim. She would be an instrument that God would use to change the direction of my life. I met her at a beer blast party at the apartment of one of my friends. After we socialized at the party for sometime I asked her if she wanted to go to my room at the frat house and she agreed. After spending some time at my room I made a move to kiss her and she said, "I don't do that sort of thing, I'm a Christian."

I was very surprised and asked, "What do you mean?"

She said, "I'm a Christian. Two years ago I gave my life to Christ and I follow Him everyday and I don't engage in sexual stuff."

I had never heard anyone my age ever talk like that before and I was very impressed. As I began to question her she revealed to me a lot about her spiritual journey. I felt very comfortable with her so I basically spilled my guts and told her all about myself and how I was trapped in so much sin. We had a great conversation that went on for hours. Through it all she kept telling me that all I really needed to do was to give my life to Christ and He would set me free. I told her that I went to Mass and Confession all the time and that I had really tried to stop sinning but had failed.

"You go to church Henry, but have you really given your entire life to God? Have you really surrendered your will to His? Have you really met Jesus on a personal level?"

Her questioning helped me to see for the first time in my life that I hadn't really met Jesus or surrendered my life into His hands. I was stirred to the very core of my being. I was being challenged to meet God in a personal way. The whole thing was intense.

We met again the next afternoon and continued our conversation about God. I was very excited because she was telling me things that seemed too good to be true. At the same time, I was also cautious because she was a Protestant. I had grown up in a completely Catholic world and anything Protestant was very strange.

After three weeks of daily conversations I could see that she and her born-again friends were the real deal; their lives were full of God's joy and peace and they weren't sinning like me. I was the party guy who the world said should be having all the fun and yet I was the one who was unhappy and unsatisfied. I wanted what they had and what they had was Jesus in their hearts.

I had learned that my Catholic faith was fine. I was the problem. The sacraments of the Church are great, but I was blocking the grace that God wanted to give me through those sacraments. *Until I surrendered my will to God, I was not going to know the power of Jesus or my*

Catholic faith. It's ironic, that a person has to surrender in order to win the victory, but that's exactly how it is with God. The thought of surrendering my entire life into God's hands was frightening to me. I was scared to let go of my life, to let Jesus direct my future. What if Jesus wanted me to be a priest and go off to Africa as a missionary? Those kinds of thoughts tormented me. At that point I wanted to follow Jesus but only on my terms because I was scared of His.

One evening I told Kim about my fear of surrendering to Jesus. I told her, "I feel like I'm a kid sitting on the living room floor and I'm playing with my toys (which were my sins) and I hear Jesus knocking on my door. You tell me that I need to open the door and let Jesus into my life, but I'm afraid that if I let Jesus in He's going to take all my toys away and I won't be happy."

Straightaway Kim replied, "Henry, you've got it all wrong. You should envision Jesus as Santa Claus out there knocking on the door and when you let Him in, yes, He's going to take away all your old, broken toys, but He's going to give you new ones that you will like much better."

The Holy Spirit must have inspired her with that answer because it just seemed to take my fear away. I told Kim that I wanted to give my life to Christ and experience the kind of relationship with Jesus that she enjoyed. She was very happy about my decision and suggested that we go to Bowling Green State University where she had a group of charismatic friends. There I could give my life to Christ, and they would pray for me to be filled with the Holy Spirit. I agreed and we made plans to go.

We couldn't go that Sunday because it was Easter and we both went home to visit our families.

New Life in the Spirit

The next weekend we drove up to BGSU on Saturday and met some of her friends. I went to Saturday evening Mass to fulfill my Sunday obligation because we were planning on going to a Protestant Church service on Sunday morning. That night I stayed with some Christian guys that were friends of Kim. When I went to bed that night I had a really awesome experience. While lying in bed, many thoughts swirled through my mind.

Suddenly my mind saw that great scene from the movie *The Ten Commandments* where all the Hebrew slaves are leaving Egypt with their wagons, children, and animals. At that moment a voice spoke to my mind. It was the voice of God and it said, *"This is your last day of slavery. Tomorrow you will be set free."*

Chills ran down my spine. I settled in for a good night's sleep.

The next morning we went to a small non-denominational chapel located on the campus of BGSU. The service began at 9:00 a.m., and it was quite different than anything that I had ever experienced. About three hundred college students packed the chapel from wall to wall. The first ninety minutes they sang songs and praised God spontaneously with up-raised hands. "Alle-luia," "Hosanna," and "Praise Jesus" rang out from every person. At times they spoke in tongues and even sang in tongues together. It sounded heavenly, and I was greatly impressed. It was evident that these people loved Jesus and loved to praise Him.

During the next ninety minutes a young minister named Peter gave a great sermon. He spoke for an hour and a half yet it didn't seem very long at all. He was full of faith and love for Jesus.

At noon the church service ended and people were socializing. One of the guys that I had stayed with the night before asked me, "Well, did you get zapped by the Holy Spirit?"

"No," I replied.

"Well, do you want to give your life to Christ?" he asked.

"Yes, that's why I came here," I answered.

He looked around and spotted a place for us to pray. At the back of the chapel was a small empty room that was normally used for chair storage. Kim, Nancy, this fellow, and myself sat on folding chairs in a small circle in that empty room away from the noise of the other people. It was a few minutes past noon on April 6, 1975, and my life was about to change forever. I didn't know what to do so the guy told me to just pray aloud and tell God that I was sorry for my sins and give my life to Jesus. I prayed the best I could.

I said, "Lord, tomorrow I'm going to be drunk, unless You do something about it because I can't. These people tell me that You can do anything, so I hope you will help me. I'm sorry for all the sins of my life. I don't know if You want a guy like me, but if You do, my life is Yours. I'll do whatever You want for the rest of my life. Please fill me with Your Holy Spirit." I prayed those words with all the sincerity, honesty, and love that I could summon.

After I finished, the other three people began to pray softly. They were praising Jesus in English and also praying in tongues. I was hoping to receive the gift of tongues which they had told me was a common occurrence for those who surrender to the Lord and ask for the Holy Spirit. We prayed for about five minutes but I didn't experience anything. Kim's friend thought this was unusual and asked me, "Did you really repent?"

I told him that I was as sorry as I could be for my sins and that I didn't know what else to do or say. He accepted what I said and he thought for just a moment, then he asked, "Have you ever had anything to do with the occult?"

"What's the occult?" I replied, because I had never heard of it.

He said, "You know, stuff like fortune tellers, horoscopes, and ouija boards. Those types of things are from the devil and they can block God's power in a person."

I told him that I had read the horoscopes in the newspaper over the years, but that I really didn't believe in them. Then, an incident came to mind that had occurred nine years before and that I had completely forgotten about until that moment. When I was in the eighth grade I went over to my neighbor's barn to play basketball with the neighbor boy who was my age. We went into the house to get a drink of water and take a break. He asked if I wanted to play with the ouija board. I replied that I had never heard of that game. He was very excited about the game and told me that it could really predict the future. I didn't believe him at all and told him so. He challenged me to give it a try so we played the game. I told him that I would prove that the game was phony. We asked the "spirits" to predict the score of the Dallas Cowboys versus the Cleveland Browns football game that was going to be played the following day. At that time the Browns were a great team while Dallas had a terrible team, so I thought the Browns would win easily. We called upon the spirits to tell us what the score would be. The game predicted that Dallas would win by a score of thirty to zero. I laughed and ridiculed my friend for his belief in such a crazy prediction. *The next day Dallas won the game by a score of thirty to zero!* I was shocked and wondered how the game could have predicted that score. But those neighbors moved away and I never encountered a ouija board again. My memory of that event had faded away until Kim's friend asked me if I ever had anything to do with the occult.

Even though it felt embarrassing to me, I explained the ouija board event to the group. Kim's friend explained to me that my participation in reading horoscopes and playing with the ouija board, even though I didn't believe in them, was wrong behavior and could be a spiritual obstacle. He told me that I needed to renounce those things which meant that I regretted my past involvement with them and that I was promising to never have anything to do with them in the future. I agreed and said a prayer renouncing any involvement with the occult.

After renouncing the occult we once again began to pray for the coming of the Holy Spirit into my life. This

My Gospel

time I experienced what Jesus had promised to the Apostles, "*You will be baptized in the Holy Spirit.*" It is impossible for me to accurately put into words what I experienced. It was the most awesome event of my life.

As I prayed it seemed that pure light was filling my entire being. The weight of the world seemed to lift from my shoulders. I *knew* that my sins were all forgiven. An immense feeling of joy and peace pervaded my consciousness that words cannot describe. I began to speak in tongues and to praise Jesus from the depths of my soul. It was impossible for me to speak a foreign language so I knew that God was working a miracle in me. That had a very profound effect upon me. To hear other people talk about God is one thing, but to experience the miracle working power of God in your own life, well, that is something totally different. I knew then that God was real and that Jesus loved me. I didn't have to depend on someone else's testimony. I now knew Jesus through my own experience. I can't adequately put into words what it was like to meet Jesus, but I knew that I had met Him and that He had accepted me as His own. It was a foretaste of Heaven.

Dear Friend, would you take a few moments right now and pray to Jesus? Ask Him to fill you with the Holy Spirit. Surrender your life to God right now and you will find true life. "*Whoever loses his life for my sake will find it.*" Jesus is speaking those words to you and to all men. It is the irony of Christianity that a person has to surrender in order to win the victory. Surrender your will, your future, your heart, along with your sins and failures. Yes, give it all to Jesus and He will accept you and forgive you and heal your soul. He will not reject you. He said, *"No one who comes to Me will I in anyway reject."* He loves you so much that He was willing to suffer torture and death on a cross so that you might be forgiven of your sins and live with Him forever in heaven. Respond to His love now; say yes to His marriage proposal. He is the Groom who wants you to be His bride forever and to live in happiness. But He will not force you to love Him. He gave you a free will and your 'yes' must be freely given with all your heart. Say 'yes' to Jesus today and cling to Him, your beloved Spouse, all the days of your life. If you're not ready yet to give yourself to Jesus, then at least ask Him to help you become ready. Ask Him to work in your heart and to prepare it for His love so that one day soon you will be able to surrender your life completely to Him. Close the book now and spend some time with Jesus.

Doubts

We prayed and praised God for about fifteen minutes. We shared hugs and tears of joy. Kim and Nancy were very happy for me and my new relationship with Jesus. Eventually we left the chapel rejoicing and went to lunch. As we were driving home that afternoon I began to experience some doubts about what had happened to me. Was I really forgiven? Was I really on my way to Heaven? Would this joy and happiness really last or would it be gone in a few days? I told Kim about all of these doubts that were attacking my mind. She smiled and said that the same thing had happened to her at her conversion. In fact, she pointed out that the same type of thing had happened to Jesus. That surprised me and she then explained what she meant.

She said, "Remember when Jesus was baptized by John in the Jordan River and God the Father spoke and said, *'This is my beloved Son in whom I am well pleased.'* Well, what was the next thing that happened to Jesus? The gospel says that the Spirit led Jesus into the desert where He was tempted. And what did the Devil say to Jesus? He said, 'If you are the Son of God, change these stones into bread.' You see Henry, the Devil tried to get Jesus to doubt what God had just said. God said, *'You are my Son,'* but the Devil said, *'If* you're God's Son.' The devil tries to do the same thing to us. You have just given your life to Jesus and He filled you with His Holy Spirit, but the devil is trying to steal you away from Jesus by trying to get you to doubt the whole thing. You just need to reject those doubts and hold fast to your faith in Jesus."

Her explanation made me feel better immediately and in a few moments all my doubts and fears were gone. We drove all the way back to Miami University praising God.

Roger's Conversion

When I arrived back home at the fraternity house that evening, I found that my friend Roger wasn't there. Roger and I had been best friends since the first grade and roommates for four years at college. Roger was out on a date, and he didn't come back to our room until 1:00 a.m.

When he came in, I immediately began to tell him all about the life changing experience that had happened to me that day. He had a Catholic background very similar to mine and everything that I said to him seemed new and strange. I really got his attention by demonstrating the gift of tongues. He knew that I couldn't speak any foreign languages, so when I spoke in tongues it really amazed him. We talked until about 4:30 a.m. as I shared my story and described the joy and peace that was flooding my soul.

Without knowing it, I had immediately become an evangelizer. One of the effects of receiving the Holy Spirit was that I wanted to share the "good news" or gospel with others. I wanted them to experience the saving power of Jesus also. From that day until the present time, I have always had a desire in my heart to bring others to Jesus so they could be forgiven, healed, and filled with the Holy Spirit. That desire to evangelize is one of the gifts of the Holy Spirit.

Roger was very interested in everything I had to say, and we continued to discuss this new life in the Spirit for the next three days. He had a lot of questions which I answered as best as I could.

On Thursday afternoon of that week, Roger came walking through the door of our room with a big smile on his face. I asked, "What happened to you?"

"The same thing that happened to you!" he replied, and proceeded to tell me the whole story.

He and a friend had driven to a nearby town to pick up his car which had been in the shop for repairs. He dropped him off at the garage and began to drive home.

While he was driving he was thinking about everything we had discussed during the last few days. He believed that it was all true and that God was calling him into a deeper relationship. A decisive moment in his life had arrived, and he felt he could no longer delay his decision. He surrendered himself completely to God and asked to be filled with the Holy Spirit.

Immediately his prayer was answered. He experienced the love of God being poured into his heart as the Holy Spirit filled his soul. He began to speak in tongues and praise the Lord as he drove down the street. He began to cry and was so overcome with emotion that he had to pull over and park the car because his tears were blinding his vision. Roger was a tough guy who prided himself on never crying, but the Lord melted his heart and gave him a new heart, one that knew the love of God. After savoring the sweetness of this experience with the Lord, he regained his composure and drove home where he told me all about it.

I was thrilled to hear that my best friend had experienced the Baptism in the Holy Spirit. I had shared my faith with him and he had converted. It was simple, just share your story with others and they will convert. I would soon find out that it doesn't always work so smoothly.

Roger and I were so excited about our new life in Christ, we wanted to tell others about it. So we went straight to a dorm room where we shared our stories with a couple of friends. Much to our surprise and dismay, their reaction was very negative. They didn't appreciate being told that they needed to repent of their sinfulness. They informed us that the way they were living was "just fine," and they didn't need to repent of anything. They thought we had become some kind of religious fanatics. They became angry and insisted that we leave.

From that experience I quickly learned that not everyone will accept the message of Jesus. That's the way it's been for these past thirty years. I've shared my faith with thousands of people and many have said, "I want that too." It is easy to lead these thirsty souls to the life-giving waters of Jesus. But many others have said, "Thanks, but no thanks." They reject the offer of Christ's love and mercy. I think that people often do this because they love their sins so much that they can't imagine life without their sins. They think that if they follow Christ they won't have any "fun" any more. Nothing could be further from the truth.

Sin doesn't bring happiness. Oh yes, I know that sin can be pleasurable. The Bible says, *"There's pleasure in sin, **for a season**."* But the seasons change in nature, and they also change in our lives. What once seemed to be fun eventually becomes slavery and death. Just ask the alcoholic or drug addict. At one time it was fun to get high or drunk, but when your family is destroyed, you're in financial ruin, and your health is gone, the fun is over. The slavery has begun.

Do you want to be a slave of your sins or do you want to be free in Christ? Jesus said, *"If the Son sets you free, you will be free indeed."* What joy there is in freedom! Turn to Jesus right now in your heart and ask him to set you free. He will! He said, *"I have come to set the captives free*." All he needs is your permission. Ask Him to set you free from those sinful habits that have enslaved you. Jesus set me free, and I'm sure He will do the same for you. After all, I'm nobody, just an average person in every way. If Jesus was willing to stoop down and pick me up, I'm sure He will do that for you too. Please extend your hand to Him. Reach out to Him right now and ask Him to pick you up and set you free from your sins. He will do it *if you will only ask*. Don't let fear or pridefulness stand in your way. If you humble yourself, the Lord will lift you up. Then you will know the joy of being set free and living in freedom.

Part II
Young Life in Christ

Father and Son

Soon after my conversion I called my Dad and told him all about it. He was thrilled, and we rejoiced in the Lord together. From that day, my relationship with Dad was great. We shared our faith with each other and grew in the Lord together. What a blessing it was to have a close, loving relationship with my Dad! Everyday when I came home from work, I would give him a big hug and tell him that I loved him and he would do the same in return. The only thing we disagreed about was that I claimed that I was the most blessed man in the world because I had him for my Father while he would claim that he was the most blessed man in the world because he had me for his son. We never did settle that dispute.

Before our conversions, Dad and I didn't have much of a relationship. There was very little communication of any importance between us. After our conversions, we spent endless hours talking about our new relationship with Jesus. It was Jesus who brought us together in a supernatural way. *"He shall turn the hearts of fathers toward their children,"* the Bible says, and it's true! Jesus can also fix marriages. Husbands and wives can truly become one in the Lord. These are some of the greatest miracles that the Lord does each and every day. He enables us to live in peace and harmony with our spouses and our families. He gives the peace that the world cannot give. When His peace lives in your heart, you will interact with everyone in the world in a different manner because of the peace that's dwelling inside you. That's why I said it's Heaven all the way to Heaven, and it's Hell all the way to Hell. Without Jesus and His peace in your heart, everyday is difficult. Nothing satisfies. You are always looking for more of something... more money, more power, more pleasure, more vacations, more freedom, more relationships, more respect, and on and on. People without God lack fulfillment and search endlessly for something to satisfy them and give their lives meaning. The mistake they're making is that they are looking for some*thing* instead of looking for some*one*, for God Himself. Since we are made in the image and likeness of God, only God Himself will satisfy us and bring fulfillment and true meaning to our lives. That kind of fulfillment transforms a person and how he interacts with all the people around him. With Christ in his heart, he can become a source of light and love to everyone he meets. No longer will he be thirsty and looking for water. Now rivers of living water will flow from within him and that water will replenish and renew the life of every person he meets. Family relationships that were dry and dying will be watered, grow, and bear good fruit. So it's Heaven all the way to Heaven.

Father Knows Best

The week after our conversions, I invited Roger and my Dad to go with me to the chapel at Bowling Green State University. I wanted them to meet these spirit-filled Christians and to experience the exciting charismatic worship that occurred in their non-denominational chapel each Sunday morning. I was very excited about going to church there again because I had never experienced anything like it before. The people there used the gift of tongues openly and often. The whole congregation would sing in tongues together and it created the most wonderful, heavenly sound. They also used gifts of prophecy and the interpretation of tongues to receive messages from the Lord. In addition, there were great testimonies and prayers for healing. The young minister, Peter, who led the worship, was a dynamic and persuasive speaker and I enjoyed listening to him.

Some of the experiences of the previous week caused me to have doubts about the Catholic Church. As we were traveling, I told my Dad that the Catholic Church was dead, and we needed to get out of it and join up with a Spirit-filled church like the one at BGSU. Immediately my Dad told me not to be so stupid. He pointed out that I was very young in the Spirit and that I didn't understand much yet. He explained that Jesus had established the Catholic Church and that it was the one true Church on earth with all the means of salvation within it. It was also the only infallible guide on matters of faith and morals. Further, it had the Holy Eucharist and all the other sacraments. He explained that all of the Gifts of the Holy Spirit were in the Catholic Church and available to all Catholics who would open themselves up to the working of the Holy Spirit. He told me that it was certainly true that sometimes Catholics acted more like God's frozen people instead of God's chosen people, but even so, it would be a deadly spiritual mistake to leave the Catholic Church. He compared the Catholic Church to a huge, mighty river. It might look as if the water is barely moving and there is not much sound but that is because the current is very deep. A small babbling brook makes a lot of noise and is fun to watch as it splashes its way along, but there's not any depth and very little power there. So it is with other churches. They lack the depth and power of the Catholic Church, even though it might not seem that way at first glance. Dad told me that I needed to stay in the Catholic Church and really learn the Faith. He assured me that if I did, I would come to see the beauty, wisdom, and holiness that could only be found there. Finally, he said, "Henry, if you and everyone else who gets filled with the Holy Spirit leave the Catholic Church, who will save the Catholics?" Dad convinced me that God wanted me to be His instrument of renewal in the Catholic Church, and I've never doubted it since. Jesus said, "*I was sent to gather the lost sheep of the house of Israel.*" His mission was first and foremost centered on the Jewish people but not completely limited to them. In a similar way, my primary focus has been and always will be to help Catholics become alive in the Spirit and on fire for Christ and His Church.

I thank God for my Dad's advice; it kept me from shipwrecking my young faith. Even though I had many doubts at that time, I followed his advice and kept seeking the truth and searching out the history and reasons behind everything that the Catholic Church teaches and practices. As the years went by, the doubts were all replaced by faith and trust in the Lord and in His Church. The beauty and wisdom of the Catholic Church is beyond anything that I could have imagined back in the early days of my conversion. In a multitude of ways, I have experienced the Spirit of Jesus in the Catholic Church. The Holy Spirit works through the Magisterium, the Sacraments, the liturgies, and the lives of the saints. The hundreds of religious orders are like a beautiful array of flowers, each with its own delicate color and exquisite scent, each giving its own praise to God. Most importantly, I have found the truth: the truth about God and His relationship to man. And that truth has set me free.

"Seek First the Kingdom of God"

We arrived at the Chapel on the campus of BGSU where I had experienced the Baptism in the Holy Spirit the week before. I introduced Roger and Dad to some of the people I had met there previously. Kim, who had led me to Christ, had also driven up to BGSU and had brought her friend Beth with her.

At 9:00 a.m. the worship began and it was great. People sang and praised the Lord with all their hearts. I have always loved to be part of a group of people who are praising God. To me, it's one of the most beautiful experiences in life. We sang hymns, sang in tongues, shouted praises, and used the gifts of the Holy Spirit for about ninety minutes. The young pastor, named Peter, preached a really good sermon.

His appearance was similar to paintings of St. Peter that I have seen. He was big and muscular with a black beard and a deep voice. He spoke very well and his sermon made a deep impression upon me. He spoke about dating and courtship, which was a very appropriate topic for a congregation of college students. He drew a triangle on a black board and labeled the top point God. The two bottom points were labeled Boy and Girl. He drew arrows from the Boy and Girl towards each other and said, "Most of you are looking for a mate in life, someone to marry and share your life. But you're going about it in the wrong way. You're going to parties and bars looking for the one you want and sooner or later you will surely find someone, but when you do, your relationship won't have God in it and you won't be happy."

Now he drew two arrows from the Boy and Girl towards God at the top of the triangle. "Instead of looking for a guy or a gal, you should be seeking to serve God to the best of your ability. All of your focus and energy should be in trying to build up the Kingdom of God on this earth. As you are seeking to do God's will in every part of your daily life, God will bring the mate that he wants for you across your path. You don't have to go out looking for someone because God will bring that person to you as you do His will. After all, didn't Jesus say, '*Seek first the Kingdom of God and everything else will be given unto you!*' Did Adam have to go searching in the Garden of Eden to find Eve? Of course not! The Bible says that God gave Eve to Adam. God will give you your spouse if He wants you to be married, as you put Him and His will first in your life. Then, when you get married, Jesus will be at the center of your relationship with your spouse and that will ensure the greatest happiness possible in your marriage. So stop chasing after someone to marry and put all of your trust in Jesus. Do His will as best you can and allow Jesus to bring your future spouse to you."

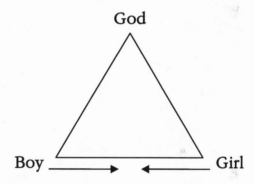

Seeking a Mate = Union without God

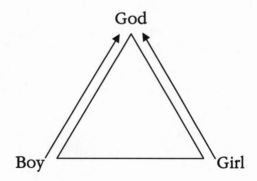

Seeking God's Will = Union with God

Wow! Those words hit me like a thunderbolt! It seemed to me that Peter had hit the bull's-eye on this topic. His words described me perfectly. I had been searching for the right girl to marry for years. I had gone about my search in the same way as most people. I had been endlessly socializing in the hope of meeting someone to marry. I took Peter's words to heart. I decided immediately that my life was going to be lived for God and that I would serve Him to the best of my ability. If God wanted me to get married, He would have to bring the right woman to me. It was settled. I wasn't going to look for a date anymore.

The next four years I threw myself into serving the Church. I organized and led prayer groups. I did lots of mission work. I tried to evangelize everyone I met. I was serving God as best as I could and was very happy as I waited for the Lord to bring me a mate.

Discerning Spirits

Kim had brought her friend Beth to BGSU so that she could be prayed over and experience the Baptism in the Holy Spirit, similar to my experience the week before. Beth was seeking a deeper union with God and was excited about the possibilities. We were expecting great things.

A group of us prayed over Beth and laid hands on her for the infilling of the Holy Spirit. We prayed and prayed, but there didn't seem to be any release of the Holy Spirit. Beth was not experiencing any Gifts of the Holy Spirit and the peace and joy of the Lord was missing. It was decided that we should take Beth to see Pastor Peter at his house.

After we had eaten our lunch, we drove over to Peter's house. I would never have guessed what was about to happen. Beth was a very beautiful woman. She had straight A's at college and was the president of a very classy sorority. Her etiquette was perfect and her fashion sense was impeccable. Who would have ever thought that this seemingly perfect coed would have a demon dwelling within her!

Peter greeted us at the door and welcomed us into his home. Beth explained how we had prayed over her but nothing seemed to have happened, and she had not experienced anything of the Holy Spirit. After only a few minutes of conversation, Peter rather matter of factly stated that Beth had a demon in her and that he would cast it out. How could he know those things? Well, he had a gift of the Spirit called the Discernment of Spirits. A person who has this gift can tell if someone has an evil spirit within them. It's quite an amazing gift.

Beth was sitting on the living room couch as Peter began to command the evil spirit to leave her in the name of Jesus. Immediately there was action. Beth fell from the couch to the floor and she began to convulse violently, to groan, and to foam at the mouth. This went on for a minute or two as Peter continued his commands of exorcism. Suddenly it was over; the demon was gone and Beth felt great. The whole thing lasted only a few minutes.

Once again we prayed that Beth would receive the Baptism of the Holy Spirit. All went smoothly this time, and she quickly experienced the Holy Spirit being poured out upon her. She received the gift of tongues and began to praise God with it. The love and joy of the Holy Spirit filled her heart and we all rejoiced together.

This experience showed me that you can't judge a book by its cover, especially in the spiritual realm. The world we live in is both physical and spiritual and everyone needs the help of God to discern spiritual realities. The natural world can be very deceptive, and we can be lulled into a false sense of security. Everyone needs to vigilantly tend to their spiritual health even more than their physical health because it is far more important. A person may look beautiful on the outside but be in a terrible spiritual condition.

In our culture, there is a great emphasis on physical health and beauty. The average person spends a lot of time and money trying to look beautiful and stay healthy, and to a degree, that's fine. The problem is the great spiritual neglect that is happening in our society that is so obsessed with beauty. Very few people spend as much time and money on their souls as they do on their bodies, and yet the soul is eternal and vastly more important. It's much more important to spend thirty minutes a day on prayer rather than on your hair. I hope that you will see the importance of your spiritual health and make a commitment to do all that you can to be spiritually beautiful for God. After all, didn't Jesus say, *"What does it profit a man to gain the whole world but lose his soul."* Listen my Friend, **life is short and eternity is forever**. Put first things first. Take care of your spiritual health and stay in the state of grace because your eternal life depends on it.

Last Days at Miami University

When someone is deeply in love all the people around them quickly notice it. The same holds true when you're in love with God. The love within you seems to come out in everything you say and do even though you're not really trying to show it. Take for example the reaction of one of my fraternity brothers the morning after my conversion. I met this brother on the stairs as I was going down to breakfast. He must have seen the joy of the Lord in my smile and demeanor because he said, "What the hell is wrong with you?" I replied that everything was just fine and continued on my way. That poor guy just couldn't understand how I could be so happy at eight o'clock on a Monday morning.

In general, people who don't know Jesus and don't love Him with their whole heart have a very difficult time understanding those who do know and love Jesus. St. Paul taught that the natural man doesn't understand spiritual realities. Boy, he was so correct.

My college days at Miami University were coming to an end. My conversion had occurred only a month before I graduated and moved home. But what a month it was! My best friend Roger had given his life to Christ and had been filled with the Holy Spirit. We went to some prayer meetings in Cincinnati and saw many spiritual gifts in action. The charismatic spiritual life seemed very new and exciting.

One thing that seemed so exciting was Scripture. Yes, Scripture! You might not think that the Bible can be thrilling, but it was to me. I read the entire New Testament within two weeks of my conversion. I just couldn't put it down because it was like God was talking directly to me and I just seemed to understand what He was saying. I had heard much of it before at church, but it was very different now. Now I knew the Author and He was living in me. I knew how the two disciples on the road to Emmaus must have felt when Jesus walked with them down the road and explained the Scriptures to them. Later they said, "*Were our hearts not burning within us as He explained the Scriptures to us.*" That's exactly how I felt each day as I read the Bible. Over the years that initial excitement has of course worn off as it must, but there is a deep love of God's Word that is a major foundational component of my life and always will be.

One morning I woke up and felt ill. I felt like I had the flu, but I didn't have a fever and I wasn't vomiting. I read for a couple of hours but felt no better. At noon I went downstairs to pick up my mail. In the mailbox I found a book that I had requested from Billy Graham. I had seen him on television and he offered to send a free book to anyone who called and I had done so.

I took the book back to my room and began to read it. The book was the exciting testimony of a woman who had survived a German concentration camp and who through God's grace was a missionary throughout Europe and even in some communist countries. At one point the woman described how she and her missionary friend both felt like they had the flu, but they didn't have a fever or vomiting. That was exactly what I was experiencing! I read on with excitement.

The two women met a pastor at a train station that day and told him about their "illness". He thought that since they had been preaching the Gospel in a communist country that they had angered the Devil and that this "illness" was being caused by demonic power. He suggested that they pray for deliverance from this evil influence right then and there in the train station. They prayed together and called down the precious blood of Jesus to cover them and protect them from all evil. Instantly they felt better and the "flu" symptoms were gone. Wow!

Immediately I thought that maybe the source of my "flu" was demonic. After all, if they had encountered demonic oppression by preaching the Gospel in an atheistic country, why should I be treated any differently when I was living in a fraternity house, which was filled with practical atheists and evils of every sort? I began to pray and to call down upon myself the precious blood of Jesus to drive away any demonic influence. Invoking the precious blood of Jesus is a very powerful prayer of exorcism. Immediately God answered my prayer. It's difficult to describe how I felt, but I will try. It seemed as if a wave of heat began at the top of my head and slowly moved down throughout my whole body and finally exited out through the soles of my feet. In just a minute it was over, and I knew that something evil had left. I felt perfectly fine and took a walk across campus to enjoy the beautiful day. The whole experience was amazing. I was learning more each day about the activity of the Evil

One and also about the superabundant power of God. St. John wrote, "*Greater is He that is in you than he that is in the world*". In my everyday life I was learning the truth of those words. The Holy Spirit dwelling in the heart of each Christian is the power of God to defeat any evil that may afflict us.

Wayne

Soon another amazing event occurred at the frat house. Wayne was a brother in the house who was a complete pothead. Dozens of the brothers took lots of drugs of all kinds. (At one time we had three drug pushers living in the house!) But Wayne was the king of the drug abusers. I really didn't like him much, and with seventy brothers living in a large house I really didn't have to associate very much with him. We rarely spoke to each other, but that suddenly changed about a week after my conversion.

One afternoon Wayne showed up at my room and said that he had to talk with me immediately. He looked like he had seen a ghost. He proceeded to tell me what had happened.

He was in the bathroom using one of the urinals when suddenly a voice spoke to him and said, "Wayne, why are you killing Me?"

He was in a state of shock because there was no one else in the bathroom! He checked the stalls but there was no one there. Where could the voice have come from? He had heard it plainly with his ears, and he was completely sober. He hadn't been doing any drugs at the time so this voice really scared him.

I asked him why he had come *to me* to talk about this. He told me that he didn't know why but that something inside of himself impelled him to talk to me specifically. He had not yet heard about my recent conversion, which made me think that this whole event was an opportunity of grace sent by God for Wayne's conversion.

We sat down and talked for the next several hours. He was really confused about God and about life. I told him the story in the Acts of the Apostles about St. Paul's conversion and how God had spoken to him in a similar way. As Paul (who was also called Saul) was traveling down the road to Damascus to arrest any Christians that he might find there, a voice spoke from Heaven and said, *"Saul, Saul, why are you persecuting me?"*

Saul answered, *"Who are you, Lord?"*

"I am Jesus whom you are persecuting," the voice replied.

I explained to Wayne how this event was the beginning of a great conversion for Saul who became one of the greatest apostles of the early church and who we know today as St. Paul. I taught Wayne that Jesus identifies Himself with every Christian and that what we do to the least of our brothers, we do to Jesus Himself. Even what we do to ourselves, if we are baptized, we do to Jesus. Wayne had been baptized as an infant, but he had really never lived a Christian life and didn't know Jesus at all.

I told Wayne that I thought it had been Jesus who had spoken to him because He said, "Why are you killing

Me." Wayne had been killing himself with drugs for years
so it was killing the life of Jesus within him. Spiritually he
was dead and God, in His infinite divine mercy, was
speaking to him and inviting him to rise from spiritual
death and receive eternal life. What a grace (gift) God
had given this lost soul. There are millions of lost souls
who never receive such a dramatic sign from God as an
audible voice from Heaven. Surely, someone must have
been praying for him.

I told Wayne all about my own recent conversion and
how God had been so merciful to me. I impressed upon
him that there are moments in life when "Jesus is passing
by," and if we miss that moment it may well be gone forever. This was one of those Bartimaeus moments. Bartimaeus was a blind beggar sitting by the road when Jesus
and a crowd of disciples passed by. Hearing the noise he
asked what was happening and was told that Jesus of
Nazareth had passed by. Jesus of Nazareth! He had heard
of His fame and how He could cure the sick. This was
his one chance to receive his sight so he shouted, *"Jesus,
Son of David, have pity on me!"*

Passersby told him to be quiet because Jesus was too
far away, but he shouted even louder. He wasn't going to
miss this opportunity which might not ever present itself
again. He didn't care what anyone thought about his
shouting; he was going to yell until he was heard. And
he was heard – by Jesus, who stopped and called him to
himself. When he was brought to Jesus, he was instantly
cured and received his sight. Then he too became a disciple.

There were so many lessons for Wayne in this story! He was spiritually blind and now Jesus had dramatically called him to Himself. I was hoping and praying that he would not miss this opportunity to surrender his life to Jesus and be filled with the Holy Spirit.

We met and talked each day for the next several days. I explained to him all that I knew about the spiritual life and the eternal seriousness involved in following Jesus. Thankfully, after several days of serious soul-searching, Wayne decided to give his life to Jesus. He understood that this would mean turning away from drugs and the whole drug lifestyle in which he had been completely immersed. He was aware that this would be a bombshell to all of his friends and that none of them would understand this change in his life. They would all probably dump him. He knew all this and yet he still wanted Jesus more. He wanted the God who had spoken to him. I was delighted.

Roger and I prayed with Wayne as he gave his life to Jesus. We prayed for the infilling of the Holy Spirit and the power of God to free him from drugs and every other sin. Our prayers were heard as he was filled with the Holy Spirit and the peace of the Lord. He was one happy man!

I don't know whatever became of Wayne and what path his life took. I only lived at Miami for two weeks after his conversion, and I never heard from him again. I do know that for those two weeks he didn't use drugs and was filled with the joy of the Lord. I believe God spoke to him, and he answered the call.

What about you my Friend? Is God speaking to you in your heart? Were you baptized as an infant but have never really known Jesus in your heart and you're not living by faith every day? Are you addicted to some kind of drug, something that you are using to try to give meaning to your life but in actuality is killing you? My Friend, Jesus is passing by right now. Shout out to him! Don't miss this opportunity! Today is the day of salvation! Pray right now and ask Jesus to heal you of everything that is wrong in your life. I'm certain that your prayer will be answered by Jesus Himself, whose heart is an infinite ocean of mercy.

In the one month I spent at college after my conversion I saw God act in many powerful ways in my life and in others, but there were also many disappointments. I shared my newfound faith with many of my closest friends but only a couple converted. Most of them thought I was strange or too religious and didn't want to go my way. As I left college and entered the world of work I kept these friends in my daily prayers. In fact, I had a mental list of eight or nine college friends that I would pray for each day as I drove to work. Each day I would pray for their conversion, that they would find Jesus and be filled with the Holy Spirit. You know what happened? Every person on that list found Jesus and had a profound conversion. Every once in a while I would hear through the grapevine that one of them had found the Lord. And I would rejoice and keep praying for the rest of them. After about four years they had all converted and were following Christ. Praise the Lord! Our prayers are very powerful and very important in the conversion of others. We must pray everyday for the conversion of sinners, especially those whom we know and love. Jesus told us that if we keep on knocking, the door will be opened, and so every day we must pray for others knowing that someday the door will open.

My Friend, who needs your prayers today? It could be your spouse or one of your children who is far from God. Maybe it's a parent or relative or a friend at work who is lost and needs to find Jesus who is the Way, the Truth and the Life. Pray for them! Pray for them! God can do infinitely more than we can in every situation. There is no person who is hopeless or a lost cause. God can transform the most hardened sinner in mere moments. History is full of such examples. Yes, my Friend, pray! Pray with all of your heart and beg Jesus to bring your friends and loved ones to Himself. If it takes many years, that's nothing when compared to eternity. If only you knew how important your prayers are in God's plan, you would pray without ceasing. When the Blessed Virgin Mary appeared to three children at Fatima in 1917, she said that many souls fall into Hell because they have no one to pray for them. Don't let your loved ones be lost forever. Instead, pray for them every day and never stop praying for them no matter what happens. Even if they die without an apparent conversion, keep praying for their soul, for who knows how God will deal with their soul in response to your prayers.

Part III
Growing in the Lord

My Gospel

In the spring of 1975 I graduated from Miami University with a B.S. degree in biological science education and had a job lined up to teach science at a Catholic junior high school in Cincinnati. That summer I lived at home and worked with my Dad on building a house for sale. My Dad was an excellent carpenter, and I had learned a lot about the trade while growing up. We worked long days, but it was great working with my Dad because we would talk about our faith in Christ all day long. It was totally amazing how our relationship was transformed by our conversions. Jesus had brought us together in a way that nothing else in the world could, and I will always be thankful for the wonderful years we spent together in the Lord.

The first day that I was home from college I ran into one of my seven older brothers. My brother Allie was filling up his truck with gas from the storage tank on the family farm. He drove a delivery truck for a local factory, but he also owned a farm and did a lot of farming. Things weren't going very well for him in farming, and he was kind of upset. He had finished gassing up the truck and was about to drive away when he said to me,

"It would take a miracle for me to make any money farming this year."

I leaned into the open window of the driver's door and replied, "I see a miracle every day."

He said, "What?"

"I pray in tongues every day. Since my Baptism in the Holy Spirit, I can speak in a language that I've never learned."

"What are you talking about?" he questioned.

So I demonstrated the gift of tongues for him by speaking in a different language for a minute or so. He was completely amazed and the look on his face showed it. I could see him take a deep swallow and then he said, "Get in the truck, I want to hear more about this."

I jumped in the truck and we went out to the field together. Then I rode with him on the tractor for the next two hours and explained to him about my conversion and my new life in the Spirit. He was very interested and wanted to know more, so the next day I rode shotgun in his delivery truck for about twelve hours and during all that time I shared "my gospel" with him. What I did that day is what we are all supposed to do all the time, which is, share "my gospel".

You may ask, "What do you mean by 'my gospel?'" Let me explain. Jesus told the Apostles "*You shall be my witnesses.*" Their job was to be His witnesses and that is our job, too, to be a witness. Well, what does a witness do? He tells the truth and nothing but the truth about what he knows, what he has seen and heard. Well, what has Jesus done for you? What power of God have you seen in your life? What has God said to you that you have heard? What is the truth about God that you know in your heart? You see, that's "your gospel." No one can argue or deny your gospel because these things happened to you. Oh, someone may say that they don't believe your testimony but don't let that shake you at all because you know that what you're saying is true because you've lived it. When you share "your gospel," it has tremendous power to touch the hearts of others because instinctively they see the authenticity in your testimony. People are naturally attracted to truth, but unfortunately we live in a world of lies. Many people have become skeptical about almost everything in our world, which is dominated by the media. Claims are constantly being made for this or that product or service that turn out to be untrue. Scams are everywhere and most everyone has been burned in some way by some sort of falsehood.

When a person starts to make claims about Jesus or religion many people are very skeptical and don't give those claims much credence. But when you tell others about all the good things that God has accomplished in your own life, that testimony has a great power to break though the skepticism and doubt that is so prevalent today. And if people can see you live out "your gospel" on an everyday basis, then there can be no doubt that "your gospel" is true.

But you might say to me, "How can I share 'my gospel' when I don't have one? I've never seen or heard God do anything in my life."

I would answer you in two ways. One, God has done many things in your life, and if you haven't seen anything, it's because you're spiritually blind. That blindness can be cured if you will turn to Jesus. Secondly, you need to start praying. Then you will start to see the power of God in your life. Pray for miracles and you will start to see some. Start living your life in Christ and He will live in you. Didn't Jesus say, *"Seek and you will find."* Well, are you seeking? Most people are seeking the things of this world so it doesn't surprise me at all that they are not finding the power of God because they're not looking for it. Start seeking God in prayer and in your actions and I guarantee that it won't be very long and you will have "your gospel" to share with others because your life will be transformed by the power of God at work in you.

After spending the entire day sharing "my gospel" with my brother Allie, I literally had no voice left. Allie pondered all that I had told him and also began to talk to Dad about this new life in the Spirit. Within a couple of weeks he decided to take the plunge and to commit his life to Christ. We prayed with him as he surrendered everything to Jesus and asked to be filled with the Holy Spirit. It was beautiful. As the Holy Spirit filled his heart, he was filled with the peace and joy of the Lord. He began to speak in tongues and to praise God in the Spirit. It was his own personal Pentecost and just like the first Pentecost, which transformed the Apostles, this Pentecost transformed Allie. Jesus said, *"I have come to cast fire upon the earth."* Well, I'd have to say that Allie caught some of that fire and has been a burning torch ever since. He's been a great witness for the Lord in his family and in society.

Faith at Work

Let me recall for you one incident of how Allie witnessed for Jesus at the factory where he worked. Some
people go to church and think that's enough. A real
Christian lives their life for Jesus twenty-four/seven, including everyday at work. A few years after his conversion Allie had a job at the factory that required him to
keep track of all of the delivery trucks and their drivers.
One day the management told him that he would have to
start keeping two sets of record books. One was to show
the authorities who sometimes checked to see if drivers
complied with state laws which limited the number of
hours they could drive without a rest. The other was to
keep track of the actual hours driven so that the drivers
would be paid accurately. Often, drivers would break the
law and drive too many hours consecutively. That was
why the management wanted two sets of records kept.

Allie told the management that he wouldn't do it. He
told them that he was a Christian and that Christians
don't lie. Keeping a false set of records to show the civil
authorities was certainly lying in Allie's estimation, and
he refused to do it.

As you might imagine a real uproar ensued. The
management couldn't believe that he wouldn't follow
orders. They tried to talk "some sense" into him, but he
steadfastly refused to lie. Then they began to threaten
him with the loss of his job, even though they hesitated
on this score because he was a long time employee who
had always worked extremely hard and was well liked by
the other employees. Eventually the crisis reached a pin-

nacle when the manager of the factory gave Allie an ultimatum – either follow orders or be demoted to one of the lower jobs in the factory. Allie stayed true to his faith and wouldn't compromise his convictions. Therefore the manager punished him by reassigning him to the loading docks where he would load trucks with other entry-level employees. The management was trying to assert their authority by making an example out of him.

But the example that Allie gave by staying true to his faith in Christ turned out to be very powerful indeed. Oh yes, it was painful for him in many ways, but God used his pain to accomplish a very great miracle – the salvation of souls. Here's how it happened.

While Allie was loading trucks, Bob, one of the young men working on the loading docks, questioned him as to why he was working there. Allie explained the whole story to him. Bob was completely amazed that someone would believe so much in Jesus that they would throw away their whole career because they wouldn't tell a lie. As the days went by, Allie was able to share his love for Jesus with Bob, and each day Bob grew thirstier for the truth that he saw in Allie.

Bob was in his early twenties and was living a wild, party-type of life even though he was a cradle Catholic. He smoked a lot of pot and even sold pot to pay for his own drug usage. He seemed an unlikely candidate for conversion but the power of a life lived for Christ is able to break through any barrier. Bob was very attracted to the truth that he heard and saw in Allie. Eventually he told Allie that he wanted to give his life to Christ. One day after work, Allie prayed with Bob right there on the loading dock as Bob surrendered his will to the will of an all-loving Father in Heaven. Bob was never the same again. His life immediately turned away from the drug lifestyle and toward God. At the time of his conversion he had a stash of pot worth about six hundred dollars. He had been planning to sell it and buy an engagement ring for his girlfriend, to whom he planned to propose. After he gave his life to Christ he realized that it would be wrong to sell it or smoke it, so he just threw it away in the trash. It was hard for him to lose all that money, but he knew that he had found something much more valuable – faith in Jesus Christ!

It's been over thirty years since Bob caught the faith from Allie. He's a wonderful Catholic husband and father with a beautiful family. He has been a great witness to many people. And what was the start of this happy ending? It was a man who wouldn't lie because of his commitment to Christ and who was willing to suffer the consequences. Because Allie was faithful to Christ, souls were saved. That's the greatest miracle of all.

Prayer Meetings

During the summer of 1975 the Catholic Charismatic Renewal was experiencing tremendous growth throughout the United States and the world. My conversion and my first spiritual experiences had been the result of my contact with Pentecostal Christians, but very quickly I heard about the Catholic Charismatic Renewal. Soon I was heavily involved in it. My Dad and I started a charismatic prayer group in our small town of Russia and invited some friends to attend. We started very small, but it grew quickly. A couple of months later we started another prayer group at a friend's home in the nearby town of Sidney, which was a town of about twenty-thousand people. Soon after we started the prayer group both of the parish priests were attending. This prayer group grew very quickly, and within a few months our Tuesday evening prayer meetings were drawing about sixty people. The group had outgrown the size of the house and we moved our prayer meetings to the Holy Angels' elementary school gym. There we had plenty of space and we could also use the classrooms to teach newcomers the New Life in the Spirit Seminar classes before the prayer meeting. Over the next ten years we had over three hundred fifty people take the New Life in the Spirit Seminar and experience the Baptism in the Holy Spirit. What a tremendous outpouring of the Holy Spirit we experienced! Lives were being transformed on a daily basis as people were surrendering their hearts to Jesus.

The Holy Angels' Prayer Group became the hub of the Catholic Charismatic Renewal in West Central Ohio. We sent out teams to give New Life in the Spirit Seminars in many parishes in the surrounding areas and to help them start prayer groups of their own. For the next four years most of my spare time was devoted to spreading the good news of Jesus' love and mercy in these prayer group activities. The rest of my spare time was devoted to missionary activity that focused on the corporal works of mercy in association with the Glenmary Home Missions.

My Dad and I had become aware of the wonderful work that the Glenmary Home Missioners were doing in the Appalachian and southern regions of the United States. These dedicated priests, brothers, and sisters were working to establish the Catholic Church in many "priest-less" counties. They were also serving the material needs of the poor in many ways. They operated thrift stores, provided food and meals, and even supervised the building and renovation of houses to provide shelter for families.

For twenty years my Dad's farm became a central drop-off location for people in a three county area. Hundreds of people would bring donations of food, clothing, building materials, and used appliances to Dad's farm where we stored these things temporarily in an empty farm building. When the building was full one of the local factories would lend us a huge truck, and we would fill it. My brother Allie would drive it down to Vanceburg, Kentucky, where the Glenmary Missioners would use it for the needs of the poor. All of this mission activity took a lot of time and effort, but we always thought it was worth it. At the Last Judgment Jesus will say, "*I was hungry and you fed Me. I was naked and you clothed Me. Whenever you did these things for the least of my brothers, you did it for Me*". We were happy to help the poor but when we hear those words at the Last Judgment, I'm sure we'll be even happier that we did those works of charity.

Public Speaking

Not long after I had moved home I met a Pentecostal fellow who was a member of a group called the Full Gospel Businessmen's Fellowship. We talked about our faith in the Lord, and he invited me to attend one of their monthly banquets. I arrived at the banquet hall to find about two hundred people who had gathered for a pot-luck dinner. Everyone was friendly and I soon felt comfortable.

But my ease was quickly about to disappear when the man who had invited me stepped up to the podium to address the crowd. After a few opening remarks he invited me to step up to the podium and share my testimony.

What! I couldn't believe that he wanted me to speak to a crowd of two hundred strangers. Obviously he didn't know that I had been scared to death of public speaking all my life. I had really hated it when a teacher had made me stand in front of the class and speak. In fact, I hated public speaking so much that for three years at college I had avoided taking the public speaking course that was required of all students in order to graduate. I was thrilled when Miami dropped that requirement my senior year, allowing me to graduate without ever taking the course. When he asked me to speak he didn't know what a trial he was about to put me through. Even though I was very fearful, I went forward to that microphone because I was extremely thankful for all that Jesus had done for me and wanted to show my gratitude. Anyway, maybe sharing my testimony would help someone else find new life in Christ.

Jesus had said, "*When they put you on trial, do not worry about what you will say for in that hour the Holy Spirit will give you the words to speak.*" Like everything else that Jesus said, those words are so true. I didn't know what to say and I didn't have anything prepared, so I just spoke from my heart and let the Holy Spirit guide my thoughts. I shared the story of my conversion and how God had filled me with the Holy Spirit. I spoke for ten or fifteen minutes and it went very well. I think that many in the audience were shocked that the gifts of the Holy Spirit had been poured out upon a Catholic. I don't think that there was another Catholic in the whole room and my testimony was something different for them, but they accepted it and me very warmly.

What shocked me was that the moment I began to speak, all fear left me. I wasn't fearful at all! To me that was a miracle! The fear was replaced by a desire to really help every person in that audience by what I was saying. I wanted my words to touch their hearts so that they would reach out to God and find the greatest treasure in the world, God's love and mercy. That desire has never left me, and I thank God for every opportunity that I have been given to speak to audiences both large and small about the greatness of God. It is one of the greatest joys of my life.

I'm still amazed at how God took away that fear of public speaking from me. I think that when we do God's will in our lives, the Holy Spirit is there to give us peace, no matter how difficult the task or duty that we are called to do. St. John wrote, *"Perfect love casts out all fear."* I know that's true, but I also know that my love is not yet perfect because I still have some fears. I pray that God will overcome my fears and weaknesses with His perfect love and strength.

What about you, my Friend? Is there some fear that holds you back from doing something for the Lord that you should be doing? I want to encourage you to trust Jesus. Put your hand into his like a child and say, "Lead me, Lord Jesus, I trust in You." I want you to know that Jesus will never let you fall as you walk with your hand in His. Go ahead. Walk with Jesus like a child.

God's Sense of Humor

There are so many things to be thankful for in my life. I'm so glad that the Lord took cursing out of my life. Before my conversion I used God's name in vain a lot. That's a very bad sin which is an insult to God and which had become a very bad habit in my life. On the day of my conversion I actually prayed that God would stop me from ever using His name wrongly again. I never wanted to insult the name of Jesus who had been so merciful to me. Since that prayer over thirty years ago I have never used the name of Jesus in a sinful manner. To me that is such a great miracle because I know that it's due to God's power and not my own because I could never control my speech. I take absolutely no credit for the removal of that vice from my life. I give all the credit to God.

I wish the removal of all my vices was that easy, but that has not been the case by any stretch of the imagination. This sinner still has a long way to go. But I do have one thing in my favor, I know that the key to holiness is God's power and not my own. That's why Jesus told the Apostles to wait and pray in Jerusalem until they received "*Power from on high.*" Our own willpower simply isn't strong enough to overcome our sinful habits. Only after the Apostles received the power of the Holy Spirit on Pentecost were they able to go out and be powerful witnesses for Christ.

Cursing is very bad but it is by no means the only way that we sin in our speech. Our tongue can be used to gossip, slander, brag, lie, abuse, blaspheme, and tear others down. We can do a lot of damage to others and ourselves with our speaking. Since God had removed cursing from my speech, I was hopeful that I could improve in other areas of speaking also. As I tried to improve I had some successes but also many failures.

One evening I prayed very earnestly, "Dear Lord, please help to be perfect in my speech tomorrow. Don't let me sin in my speaking for one day." I was determined that for at least one day I would be perfect in this one area of life.

When I woke up the next morning, I discovered that I couldn't speak at all!! I had gone to bed perfectly healthy, but the next morning it was like I had a terrible case of laryngitis even though I still felt fine. I just couldn't speak. I laughed to myself and concluded that God had heard my prayer. I guessed He figured the only way I wouldn't sin in my speech was to make sure I couldn't speak! The laryngitis lasted just one day and the following day my voice was back to normal. Someone once said, "Be careful what you pray for, because you just might get it." Oh, how true that is.

Horoscopes

The devil doesn't like it when Jesus sets us free from our old sinful habits so he tries to pull us back repeatedly into our old sins. During the summer after my conversion I played on a young men's slow-pitch softball team one night a week. It was good exercise and a lot of fun. One evening as we were getting ready for the game some of my teammates were talking about horoscopes. One of the guys was really excited because he said that his horoscope had come true that day. He had even clipped it out of the newspaper and was passing it around for us to read. I wouldn't read it and advised him to stop reading horoscopes because they are part of the occult and as Catholics we are forbidden to participate in occult practices because it is a form of idolatry. I also tried to reason with him by explaining that anyone could write some sort of generic prediction and if millions of people read it in the newspapers, it would certainly come true for at least a few people. It's just a matter of statistical averages and not some sort of spiritual power to see into the future.

My teammate seemed kind of upset with me and went off to tell the amazing power of horoscopes to some other guys. I find it very sad that so many people today look for spiritual answers in the world of the occult. We see advertising for occult and new age types of religion everywhere. Almost every newspaper prints a horoscope. Books stores have whole departments dedicated to occult/new age materials. Millions of people are sucked into this stuff and most of them have no idea that it is a form of idolatry and is very destructive to true faith in God. I only became aware of this evil at my conversion. Here the devil was pushing it right in my face again and saying look, it's really true. Thankfully, I didn't fall for the bait, and over the past thirty years I've steered clear of all areas of the occult.

The Occult

But some people I know have not been so wise and have paid a heavy price for their occult participation. I knew a lady who had been a faithful member of our prayer group for several years and really loved the Lord. Somehow she started reading some occult materials. Soon she proclaimed that she had the gift of "automatic writing" and that the "spirit" would move her to write beautiful "revelations". She claimed that her soul could travel to other worlds where she met with "spirit masters" who taught her spiritual truths. We tried to dissuade her from these practices and to explain that these phenomena were tricks of the Devil. She wouldn't listen to us and claimed that we were not "spiritually advanced" enough to understand her. I have lost track of this woman but the last report I heard about her, she had quit the Catholic faith and no longer believed in Christ.

Oh my Friend, the occult is very dangerous to our faith. You must stay away from it and not even mess around with it "for fun". Oh, yes, it is a far worse sin to place any kind of faith or belief in occult practices than to merely participate in them such as reading your horoscope in the newspaper. But even just playing around with these things out of curiosity is exposing oneself to the near occasion of sin. That is exactly how belief in such practices takes root, like in the case of my softball teammate. If he hadn't been reading it out of curiosity for fun, he would never have started to believe that it was true for him.

Occult bondage can start in what might seem to be the most innocent and harmless activity. For example, I had a former high school student who came back to visit the school some years after he graduated. He spoke to me after school and told me a chilling story of how he had spent several years deeply involved in witchcraft. He described some of the terrible evils that he had been involved in and how it had almost cost him his physical and spiritual life. Thanks be to God, he had been able to escape from this diabolical trap. He had returned to the Catholic faith to which he was now deeply committed because he knew how important the true faith was for his salvation. He urged me in the most serious terms to "keep on telling your students to stay away from the occult" in order to spare them from the hell that he had barely survived.

Then he told me how his involvement in witchcraft had begun. He said, "You'll laugh when I tell you, but it's the truth. I liked watching an old television show called

Bewitched and I watched it every day." He thought, "Wouldn't it be really cool to be able to use spiritual power to actually make things happen the way you want them to?" From that beginning he began to read books on witchcraft and all the rest followed. He had become a true believer that parents should be very careful about what they let their children watch, read, and play, to make sure there's no evil influence. In the media-saturated world in which we live today, that's a difficult job for parents which demands a lot of effort to do well, but it's absolutely essential to protecting our children from spiritual poison.

We must be vigilant throughout our life because even when we are older the Devil still tries to poison us with the occult. I knew an elderly Catholic lady who was diagnosed with cancer. She took all the medical treatments available and used the sacraments of the Church including the Anointing of the Sick. She prayed very much to be cured but nothing helped and she continued to deteriorate. Fearing death she made a desperate decision – she prayed to the Devil! She asked the Devil to cure her cancer since neither God nor medicine had done so.

Immediately, she saw great improvement and soon the doctors declared her cancer in remission. Physically she was doing great, but spiritually she was dead. Her conscience tormented her daily because she knew that she had damned her soul to save her life. After two months she couldn't take it anymore and truly repented of her sin. She went to confession and confessed everything, begging Jesus to forgive her for having turned away from Him and to the devil. She left confession at peace with God and full of joy. Immediately, the symptoms returned and soon the doctors said that her cancer was active again and they thought it would be terminal.

For the next several months she was tempted to turn to the Devil for relief, but she didn't. Her relationship with Jesus now meant more to her than life itself, and she refused to turn to anyone but Him for help. For many months she suffered terribly and things looked very bleak. Then, quite unexpectedly, the cancer went into remission. She had passed the test. She had not given up her faith in Jesus, and she lived cancer free for quite a few years until she died in the peace of the Lord.

My dear Friend, please do not turn to the occult or the Devil for any kind of power or information that you think you need. God has infinite power and knowledge. If you need help, ask God, for He can do anything you need. If He doesn't do what you want, it's because it's not in your best interest even though you might think it is. That's when you must trust that God loves you and always does what is best for the salvation of your soul. If you want to know something, ask God, for he knows all things. If God does not tell you what you want to know, then you will have to trust that it's in your best interest for you not to know at that time. Maybe God will reveal the answer later or maybe only in Heaven. But you can be sure that if God wants you to know something, He will tell you; you don't have to run off to the occult to learn the past or the future. The lying spirits of the occult will only give you lies anyway, but you'll be tricked into believing it's all true.

My dear Friend, God's Word and Holy Mother Church both explicitly command us to stay away from any contact with the Devil or the occult because it leads to death for your soul. Heed this warning and live.

Jesus Appears

One evening my friend Steve and I were having a coke at the local diner when Jack, a friend of ours, happened to see us. He lived only a few blocks away and invited us over to his house to have a steak dinner with him and his wife Sarah. The invitation seemed great but very unexpected. Jack explained that he had invited a married couple to dinner, but they had just called and said they couldn't make it. He said the steaks were already on the grill, so why not come over. We were very happy to accept his invitation and went straight to his house. It was a great meal and the four of us sat around the table socializing. I thought that it would be a good time to share with Jack and Sarah my conversion story and invite them to come to the prayer meeting that I had started.

As I was telling them about my conversion, Sarah's face suddenly changed expression. Her eyes grew wide open and she looked frightened. This lasted for about ten seconds and we asked her what was wrong. After regaining her composure she stated that I had disappeared and that someone who looked like Jesus had appeared sitting in my place. After a few moments, "Jesus" disappeared and all was back to normal. She was seated straight across the table from me and said there was no mistake about what had happened. The whole thing seemed surreal to them. They were at a loss to explain what had happened, but immediately I knew.

You see at that time in my life I had been praying every morning that I would be a good witness for Jesus and bring everyone closer to him. I would pray, "Dear Jesus, You must increase and I must decrease. Today, let people see You, not me. Let them hear You, not me. Let them touch You, not me." I prayed that way with all of my heart because I really wanted to bring others to know Jesus, but I never thought that Jesus would answer it literally by appearing in my place. But that is exactly what happened.

I explained to Jack and Sarah that what had happened was a literal answer to my daily prayer. I stressed the point that God was really trying to get through to them because he had done such an unusual thing in order to help them believe the message that I was sharing with them. We talked for a couple of hours, and I invited them to come to the prayer meeting to the learn more about the new life in the Spirit.

My Bad Example

Several months passed, but Jack and Sarah had not come to the prayer group even though I had invited them a couple more times. They said they would think about it and I was hoping they would come, but then I really dropped the ball. It happened this way.

Jack and I played together on a young men's basketball team. During one game I completely lost my temper with the referee and insulted him greatly. He promptly called a double technical foul on me and threw me out of the game. I left the court and sat down on the bench next to Jack. He turned to me and said, "So that's what it means to be a Christian!"

I was never so humiliated in all of my life. His words pierced straight through my heart. My bad example had just ruined everything that I had tried to tell him about Jesus. Immediately I saw my sin very plainly and confessed to Jack that I was completely wrong in how I had behaved. I told him there was no excuse for my bad behavior and asked him to look past my actions and look to Christ. But I had blown it. He never did come to the prayer group and, in a way, I don't blame him.

That night I was very upset with myself. I asked Jesus to forgive me, but I knew that that wasn't enough. My bad temper had to change. I only lost my temper when I was playing basketball which was my favorite activity in life. So I decided that I wouldn't play any basketball for one year from that day and that if I ever lost my temper again after that, I would give it up for life. It was a hard thing to do, but it was necessary and turned out to be very good for me.

Winning souls for Christ is more important than basketball or anything else that you might love in this world. If something in this life is causing you to give a bad example or is holding you or someone else away from Jesus, you must give it up immediately. It's as simple as that. Don't make excuses, just walk away from it, now! As a Christian your example is the loudest gospel you preach and it drowns out any other gospel you speak. As

St. Francis of Assisi would say, "Preach the Gospel always and if you have to, use words." Our lives are a powerful message for good or for evil, and the salvation of souls hang in the balance. Do your very best to give that good example that will lead you and others to Heaven. Jesus died on the cross so that your friends and family could go to Heaven. Surely, the least you can do is to make sure that your bad example doesn't lead astray those precious souls for whom Christ died. May God help you right now to make the changes in life that you need to make so that people will see Christ in you.

Heartbroken

As summer of 1975 came to an end, it was time for me to start the teaching position that I had taken at a Catholic elementary school in Cincinnati, which was about one hundred miles from my hometown. In the middle of August, I moved into a cheap apartment and began to put my classroom in order.

The first week of school did not go well. I was teaching junior high science to more than two hundred children each day and the task was overwhelming me. Normally, the first year of teaching is hard for anyone, but I had some other issues that really devastated me.

For one thing, I was terribly homesick, which really surprised me because I had been living at college for the previous four years and had not been homesick at all. My best hometown friend, Roger, had been my roommate for four years at college, but now I was living in a barren apartment on a treeless street in a large city where I didn't know anyone. The homesickness that I endured was a very painful experience.

The second and decisive blow to my mental and emotional stability came on Labor Day weekend when I drove to Cleveland to see my girlfriend Denise. We had not seen each other for an entire year because she had been in Europe at Miami University's branch campus in Luxembourg. We had met at Miami during the spring quarter when I was a junior and she was a sophomore. Our relationship seemed perfect, and we had so much fun together that spring. Being young and in love is one of the greatest experiences in the world.

It can also lead to a very painful heartache. Right before the school year ended, Denise told me that the week before we had met each other she had made a commitment to spend the next year in Europe and that she had to follow through on her plans. Wow, that was really terrible news to me because she would be gone my whole senior year. I understood that it was a great opportunity for her to go to Europe and I didn't blame her a bit for going, but it still hit me pretty hard.

During my senior year we wrote letters to each other and kept up with what was going on in our lives. From her letters I could tell that we were moving in opposite directions. Of course I wrote and told her all about my conversion and the power of the Holy Spirit in my life. In her letters she was telling me how living in Europe had set her free from old traditional values and morals. When she told me how "liberating" it had been to go topless on the French Riviera beaches, I knew that she wasn't the same person anymore. But I was still in love with her and was hoping that when she came home I would be able to convince her to give her life to Christ. That's what I was praying for as I drove to Cleveland.

I spent that Labor Day weekend with Denise at her parents' home. From the first moment it was obvious that things were not the same between us. How could they have been? My whole life had turned radically toward Christ and my every thought, word, and deed was now empowered by the Holy Spirit. Conversely, she had pretty much lost the Catholic Faith and had embraced a basically libertarian philosophy of life which allowed her to do whatever she pleased.

For two days I tried my best to convince her about the truth of Jesus and the power of His Spirit and the beauty of the Catholic Faith, but it was all to no avail. She didn't want any part of it.

By the end of the weekend the painful truth was plain to see – our relationship was over. We said our goodbye and I drove a very long, sad journey back to Cincinnati. Not only had I lost the girl I loved, but also I was very worried that she might lose her eternal soul. I shed a lot of tears that day.

The reality of the break-up was painful, but it shouldn't have been very unexpected. After all, didn't Jesus say, "*I have come to bring division on earth. From now on a house shall be divided, father against son and mother against daughter.*" What Jesus meant was that our faith in Him makes all the difference in the world and will be the dominant factor in all of our relationships. If two people in an intimate family relationship don't share a common faith in Jesus then there's going to be trouble.

Our faith in Jesus makes us take positions on very important matters that those who do not have faith will violently disagree with. A true Christian lives his faith twenty-four/seven, and it affects how he approaches everything in life. It's nearly impossible for such a person to live in harmony with someone who approaches everything in life from a different worldview. The constant conflict will eventually destroy any natural attachment or attraction the two people may have had and the end result will be a separation.

My dear Friend, if you are unmarried at this time, this is a very important concept for you to understand and embrace. When looking for a future spouse, you must place your faith in Christ as your top priority, and sharing a common faith must trump any other considerations. I'm sure you want to have a happy marriage and live to a ripe old age in peace and harmony. Do you think that such a wonderful marriage will happen if you make bad choices leading up to your marriage? I can assure you that bad choices will lead to misery. Therefore it is imperative that you commit your life and your whole heart to the service of Jesus and to live out your Catholic faith in a diligent manner. Then you must make an ironclad, unbreakable resolve that you will only marry someone who is a truly committed Catholic like yourself. Guard your heart and do not let yourself fall in love or become infatuated with someone who does not measure up to your religious standards. Don't worry about meeting such a person or that your standards are too strict. God is in control of your life and He is quite able to bring the perfect person to you to be your spouse. If He doesn't, then you will know that it's God's will for you not to marry. You must always trust in God and be at peace knowing that God's will for you will make you the happiest person that you can be both here and in the next life. Many people have made a complete wreck of their lives by not really having any religious standards to evaluate prospective mates, and so they marry someone they happen to fall in love with even though that person is not a good choice for long-term stability and spiritual unity. Inevitably, these marriages fall apart in one way or another and the persons involved end up quite unhappy.

My dear unmarried Friend, I hope you realize that you will be far happier following Christ's way of living and never marrying rather than lowering your religious standards and marrying someone who is really a poor choice. I really hope you take this advice to heart and live by it.

For many years I prayed each day for Denise's conversion, but I don't know whatever happened in her life. Hopefully, she has found true happiness in Christ.

That Labor Day Weekend break-up caused me great sadness. Combined with homesickness and an overwhelming new teaching job, I felt I was at the breaking point. I didn't want to have a nervous breakdown because I had an older brother who had experienced a nervous breakdown and I had seen the devastating effects of it in his life. So I made the decision to quit my job and move back home. In some ways I felt like a failure, and it was somewhat humiliating, but I felt that I had to do it to preserve my mental health.

At this point you might say, "I thought you said, 'It's Heaven all the way to Heaven'. Your experience doesn't sound very heavenly at this point!" Well, in a way you have a good point. Losing my girlfriend, quitting my job, and having to move back home were certainly painful experiences, but Jesus was with me through it all, and that's the key. Jesus didn't promise a pain-free life. In fact, He promised His followers that they would suffer. He said, *"In the world you will have many trials, but be of good cheer, for I have overcome the world."*

You see, we can be of good cheer even in the midst of our suffering because Jesus, the almighty God, is with us. I can attest that at that very painful time in my life, Jesus was with me and He comforted me, sustained me, and interiorly healed me in truly profound ways. In fact, as I look back over the years, I see that it was in those painful experiences that I learned the greatest lessons and came to know the deepest love.

Back Home and a New Job

Dad and Mom were sympathetic to my situation and allowed me to move back in with them. I needed a job in order to repay my college loans, but the economy and job market in 1975 were pretty bad. I took the first job I could find, which was working as an assistant maintenance man for the county. It was a very easy job and the pay wasn't as bad as you might think. In fact, my salary was higher than my salary had been as a Catholic schoolteacher with a B.S. degree. (That's a rather sad commentary on the value our society and our Church places on teachers.)

This new job turned out to be a great benefit to my spiritual growth in two ways.

First, it allowed me a lot of time to read. I had to be at work by 6:00 a.m. to turn on the boilers for the courthouse and the jail and to answer the phone, which seldom rang. Those were my only duties until the chief maintenance man arrived at 10:00 a.m. That allowed me about four hours each morning to sit undisturbed and read, and did I ever take advantage of it! Over the next eighteen months I read more than one hundred books on religion and spirituality. I was like a sponge soaking up as much wisdom and knowledge as I could about the Lord and the Catholic Church. All of this reading really helped me to understand the Faith. I think it's very important for every Catholic to really understand what the Church believes and why. If you don't know Church teaching very well, you won't be able to pass it on to others. And even if you know doctrines, but you don't know why they are true, then you will have no credibility when others are skeptical and question you about your beliefs.

It's a sad fact that millions of Catholics have been convinced to leave the Catholic Church and to join various Christian denominations and even non-Christian religions. This happens because there are many Catholics who don't really know what the Church believes and why. I'm convinced that a Catholic who really understands the Faith would never leave the Church. The Catholic Church has the fullness of truth and the fullness of the means of salvation. Once a person understands that fact, then there is really no legitimate reason to go anywhere else.

Because I had so much free time at my job it made it very easy to study the Faith. Most people don't have such an opportunity and have to make an effort to find the time to do spiritual reading. But knowing the Faith is essential. Therefore, every Catholic must arrange his daily schedule so that there is some time for spiritual reading. Actually, most people waste quite a bit of time everyday. All that is necessary is a little discipline in order to change some of that wasted time into beneficial spiritual reading. It is well worth the effort.

The second way that the maintenance job helped my spiritual growth was that I had to deal with small persecutions for my faith. Persecution either makes a person stronger or it makes you run, hide, or quit. I wasn't about to do the latter, so I had to get stronger and make my sword sharper.

Tom was the chief maintenance man, and the two of us worked together everyday fixing things at various county facilities. He was a Catholic who really didn't practice the Faith very much. He didn't follow many of the moral teachings of the Church because they were inconvenient or simply because he liked to sin. For example, he liked pornography and had a picture of a naked woman on his desk calendar. I came to work earlier than he did and everyday I would turn it over so it couldn't be seen, and everyday when he arrived he would turn it back and cuss at me. I would then tell him to repent, and he would cuss at me some more. That's how the day started and it usually went downhill after that.

I guess my zeal for the Lord acted like a conscience that Tom had long ago quit paying attention to. But unlike the voice of his own conscience, he couldn't ignore me. So he decided to ridicule me – all day long. It really got old, but it made me tougher and that's a very good thing for a Christian. Anyone who really follows Christ is going to be ridiculed by the world. Jesus said, *"If you were of the world the world would love you, but since you are not of the world, therefore the world hates you."* Since the world hates us we had better toughen up, and small persecutions, like ridicule, are perfect training.

So looking back on it all now, that job was a real blessing and just what I needed in my young spiritual life. It gave me time to read and learn my faith very well. Then it tested my faith with daily persecutions that made me put knowledge into practice. God was teaching me and testing me daily in the ordinary routine of life. I think He does that for all of us if we are able to recognize it.

Learning to Love

After a year and a half working at the maintenance job I was able to get a new job. Shelby County was beginning a program for the mentally retarded and developmentally disabled people of the county. There was going to be a school for the children and a sheltered workshop for the adults. I was hired as part of the original staff of the adult workshop where I functioned as a floor supervisor. I had to supervise the work activities of approximately fifteen adults who were severely retarded or disabled. I also took care of all their personal needs throughout the day including the administration of medicine, helping with their lunch, and assisting their needs in the bathroom.

The world of the mentally retarded was a whole new world to me. I had very little contact with mentally retarded people when I was growing up and really didn't know what to expect. The first couple of weeks on the job were difficult for me. It took a lot of patience and understanding to deal with the myriad of problems that occurred almost continually. Many of the clients seemed downright repulsive to me, and I wondered if I was suited for the work. Then something happened that changed everything.

Sandra was one of our clients. She was probably in her late thirties and had multiple mental and physical problems. She was very short, skinny, and terribly humpbacked. One hip was far higher than the other and she walked with a terrible limp. Her face was contorted and twisted and her smile revealed very irregular teeth. When I looked at her I was repulsed because she was a tangled mess of humanity.

But she was not repulsed by me. In fact, she liked me. Each morning after being dropped off by the bus, she would limp her way through the front door, come right to me, and give me a big hug saying, "Good morning, Henry." I always replied politely but inside I was very uncomfortable. I felt like saying "Someone get this freak off of me!" I know that sounds terrible, but that's how I felt at the time. I knew in my head that I should love all people, but applying that concept in this situation just wasn't happening for me.

One evening I was reading a book about Mother Teresa of Calcutta, a person that I admired very much. There I read that Mother Teresa would instruct her sisters about how they should treat the poor. She told them to observe how the priest at the altar treats the Sacred Host. How he lifts it carefully and holds it up with the greatest respect and reverence. He treats the host with so much love and reverence because it is the Body of Christ; it is Christ Himself. Today you sisters will go out into the streets and you will find the sick and the dying, people with sores who smell awful, or are half-eaten by worms and covered in filth and rags. You must pick up that man with the same love and reverence that the priest has when he picks up the Sacred Host at Mass, because you too are picking up the Body of Christ. In that man you are picking up Christ Himself because He said, "*Whatever you do to the least of My brothers, you do to Me.*" So love that man the way you love Christ. Show that love in how you carry him, how you touch him, how you speak to him, and how you look at him, for in loving him you are loving God Himself.

Her words hit me like a ton of bricks! I closed the book and began to think about Sandra and all the other clients. I certainly was not treating her like I treated the Holy Eucharist. At that time in my life I was able to go to Mass every morning because my job didn't start until 9:00 a.m. Everyday I would go to Holy Communion and receive Jesus with all the love and reverence that my pitiful heart could muster. I had no difficulty believing that the Holy Eucharist was truly the Body and Blood of Christ.

Mother Teresa's Eucharistic analogy really pierced my mind and heart. From that moment the grace of God changed something inside of me. I think the Holy Spirit just poured the love of God into my heart. From that moment I had a completely different attitude towards Sandra and all the other clients. The next day they were all still the same, but I was different.

When Sandra gave me her good-morning hug and greeting, I embraced her as if she were Jesus with all the love in my heart. I held her as if I was holding the Sacred Host of Holy Communion. There are moments that can change a person forever, and that was certainly one for me. It's been thirty years since that tiny, twisted, disfigured little saint embraced me and gave me a heart transplant. Through Sandra, God took out my stony heart and gave me a new, soft, human heart. Even now as I write these words, the tears are streaming down my cheeks as I am overcome with emotion.

Sandra and all those other "special" people taught me so much during the four years that I worked at S&H Products. In their own way they taught me how to love unconditionally. What a great gift! What could be better!

In general, the world we live in does not recognize the tremendous contribution that the mentally retarded and developmentally disabled make to our society. By just being themselves, with all of their incredible neediness, they demand our unconditional love. They drag it out of us every moment of the day. They make us all more human in the true sense of the word. That's why

God allows these afflictions. So that He can bring even greater good from them, and that greater good is unconditional love.

Many people today want to look the other way when they encounter God's special ones. It's too painful to look at them. It's too much work to help them. It's just too demanding and all of the efforts won't cure them anyway. Some want to use science to manipulate human genetics and reproduction in order to prevent them; others want to abort them. It's cheaper and easier they say. Still others want to warehouse them away from the mainstream of society. Out of sight, out of mind.

All of these attitudes indicate a fear of unconditional love, a love that responds simply because there's a need, and the one who is in need is Jesus. Dear Friend, do not be afraid of unconditional love. Instead of running away from it, embrace it. Pull it close to yourself and you will be transformed. Open your heart to the unconditional love that Jesus has for you, and then you will be able to love others because of His love dwelling in you. You can't give what you don't have, and you can't give unconditional love if you haven't first received it from God.

Look at yourself; you're a very needy person in so many ways. Compared to God you are small, twisted, disfigured, and completely helpless. And with all of your sins, Jesus embraced His cross for you, so that you might live. That was His unconditional love for you. Now let His love for you flow out to others. Every family with a special child knows what I am talking about. The child with tremendous needs seems to claim the love of his father and mother in a more powerful way than the other children. The constant care and attention creates un-breakable bonds of love and affection, far beyond the normal. Very often these parents come to realize the special gift that they have been given in their special-needs child. They are no longer afraid of unconditional love, for God has taught them the beauty of this love through their own child.

Part IV
Signs and Wonders

Healings

Those first few years after my conversion were a whirlwind of activity. All of my time was occupied with my job, charismatic prayer meetings, mission work, praying, reading, and some sports. Those prayer meetings were really great.

I love to praise the Lord, and the charismatic prayer meetings gave me a unique way of expressing my love for God. It was also a way to experience in a very tangible and dramatic fashion the power of the Holy Spirit at work today in the lives of believers. Over the years I've heard hundreds of people tell me about the great things that God had done in their lives. I saw the power of God in response to our prayers time and again. Let me recall for you just a few stories of God's love and power that I experienced in the charismatic renewal.

On two different occasions I experienced instantaneous physical healing. The first healing occurred after I had strained my back carrying an electric range up a flight of stairs. I had injured my back numerous times before and it always took quite a while to get back to normal. But on that day there happened to be a charismatic healing Mass scheduled for that evening at a church in Dayton, which was forty miles away. My dad planned to go, but I was going to stay home because my back hurt so badly that the car ride would be excruciating. Dad was persistent in urging me to go because after all, it was a healing Mass and I definitely needed healing. Finally, I agreed to go. The drive there was very painful as expected, and I dreaded the ride home.

The Mass was great and filled with lots of exuberant praise and worship. After Communion there was a quiet time and if someone in the congregation had a message in tongues or a prophecy they could approach the microphone at the front of the church and speak to the congregation. A woman went forward and spoke a prophecy. The first words really got my attention. "I am your Lord and God and I want to heal you."

When I heard those words I immediately prayed quietly saying, "Dear Jesus, please heal me." The moment I whispered those words I began to feel the healing power of God. It was like a bar of heat that rolled down from my shoulders to the bottom of my back. It took about ten seconds. After that I was perfectly healthy and had no pain whatsoever. When Mass was over, I immediately stepped out of the pew into the aisle and did toe touches. I could move freely with no pain. I had been healed and was overjoyed. I shared this wonderful news with the people there, and we all thanked and praised God.

I have injured my back many times since that day and repeatedly had to get medical help. I thank God for my chiropractor who has helped me many times. Only on that one occasion was I cured instantly through prayer, and I don't know why. I guess it was just a kiss on the cheek from God.

A few years later I was serving on a team that was directing a charismatic conference which focused on the Blessed Virgin Mary and her role in our salvation. It was a three-day conference held at the University of Dayton and about five hundred people attended. As you can imagine I was very busy fulfilling my various duties.

My biggest problem was that I was very sick with a good old-fashioned cold and sore throat. Each swallow felt like razor blades in my throat. I really just wanted to go to bed, but I had important duties that I felt I had to fulfill so I just kept on going.

We had scheduled prayer teams to be in two classrooms during the Saturday lunchtime and to pray for healing for anyone who wanted prayers. I went to one of the classrooms and stood in line for my turn. I entered the classroom and a man and woman prayer team welcomed me and asked me what I wanted them to pray for. I told them that I had a terribly sore throat and wanted healing. As they began to pray the woman touched my throat with some blessed oil. The moment she touched me all my pain left! It was amazing! I mean, it left in one second! They had just begun to pray when I interrupted and told them that I had already been healed and there was no need to ask anymore. Instead we spent the next five minutes praising God and thanking Him for His healing power. When I left, I told those waiting in line about my healing and that they should be ready for a miracle.

The rest of that weekend I felt perfectly fine and fulfilled all my duties with the conference team. Once again,

I have to say that healing is a mystery to me. I don't
know why God cured me instantly on that day, and He
has not cured me when I've had colds and sore throats
on other occasions. What I do know is that sometimes
Jesus does cure physical illness instantly. Miracles of healing actually do happen, and I think we should always
pray for healing. Don't get me wrong, I'm not against
doctors and medicine. Quite the contrary, I thank God for
all the wonderful people who serve God in the healing
professions. The work they do is truly a work of mercy
and God will bless them for it. But it is a good thing to
join prayer to everything we do, and it's a good thing to
join prayer to all of our efforts to heal. Sometimes God
just takes over and heals a person instantly. I've seen it
happen to others many times, and it has happened to me
twice.

Holding Back the Rain

I've gone several times to the National Charismatic
Conference held at Notre Dame University. Tens of thousands of charismatic Catholics join together for a three-
day weekend of prayer, praise, teaching, and fellowship.
At these awesome conferences I've seen some pretty
amazing things.

One year our prayers stopped the rain. It had rained
throughout Friday and Saturday. On Friday evening, thirty
thousand people had sat in the rain in the football stadium and listened to two speakers for about three hours.
Of course it was uncomfortable, but we offered up the
inconvenience. When Saturday evening's conference at

the stadium began we were facing another three hours of steady rain. A man who spoke for the leaders of the conference told the crowd that it was their opinion that God would stop the rain during the first speech if everyone prayed. So the whole crowd began to pray aloud and ask God to stop the rain. About thirty seconds later the rain which had been falling steadily all day suddenly stopped. It was like turning off a faucet and the crowd just went wild. A roar of approval echoed up to the heavens.

The speaker gave an excellent talk, but I don't remember anything he said. What I do remember is that the moment he finished and sat down the rain began to fall. The music ministry played some songs, and we sang our praises in the rain for about thirty minutes.

The conference leader came back to the microphone and told the crowd that God had given us exactly what we had asked for. We had prayed for no rain during the speech, and that's what had happened. But there was another speaker scheduled to talk so he said that we should all pray again. So thirty thousand voices once again asked God to stop the rain for the next speech. Once again the rain stopped in an eerily sudden fashion! If anyone had entertained doubts the first time, those doubts were erased. It just couldn't be a coincidence that the rain stopped at the precise moment we prayed. No, we were witnesses to the power of God over nature, and it made a deep impression upon all who were there. In fact, the rain phenomenon is the only thing I remember about that conference. At that moment we had a taste of what the Apostles felt when Jesus calmed the storm on the Sea of Galilee. It was awesome and once again the crowd went wild with praises to God.

The moment the second speaker finished and sat down the rain began yet again. We didn't care. We laughed and sang some more songs. We knew that God was with us and that He could do all things. His power had been very evident that evening.

Rise and Walk

At another Notre Dame conference we had a young woman in our group who was experiencing a lot of pain in both of her legs. She was in so much pain that when it was time to go to the evening general session she decided to stay in her room rather than undertake the long walk to the stadium. We felt bad for her and decided that we should pray for healing. We laid hands on her and prayed. Within a few minutes God answered our prayers, and she was pain free. She walked with us almost a mile to and from the stadium that evening without any pain. God touched her legs and her heart that day. The physical healing really helped her accept the fact that God loved her with an unconditional love, which was something she had struggled with previously.

Food Miracle

The most astounding miracle we experienced at Notre Dame was the physical multiplication of food. Yes, you read that correctly, the multiplication of food!

That year Fr. Rick Thomas brought some very poor Mexicans to the conference for the purpose of testifying to the miracles that they had witnessed in Juarez, Mexico. Fr. Rick had started a food ministry which served the starving people who lived in the city dump in Juarez. On numerous occasions God had multiplied food right before their eyes in order to feed overwhelming numbers of people that Fr. Rick was not prepared to feed. You can read all about these marvelous events in a book called *Miracles in El Paso?* by Fr. Rene Laurentin. These Mexicans spoke to the crowd through an interpreter and told how they had seen food multiplied like in the miracle of the loaves and fishes. Their testimony was very powerful.

It was Sunday at noon, and people were eating lunch. Some went to the cafeteria while others got lunch elsewhere. The Mexican men were sitting in a group on the lawn between some campus buildings. I saw them as I was carrying some luggage for an elderly lady out to her car in the parking lot. The Mexicans stopped three men from our group who were passing by and in their broken English they asked where they could find Fr. Rick because he had their meal tickets. My friends had no idea where to find Fr. Rick, but they offered the Mexicans the food they had left over from their own lunches, which was two sandwiches and three cans of Pepsi. It was certainly not enough for a dozen men, but they were happy to get it.

To my friends' amazement they placed the food on the grass and stood in a circle extending their hands over it and began to pray in Spanish. My three friends couldn't understand what they were saying but guessed that they were asking God to multiply the food. One happened to have an audio tape recorder with him so he turned it on.

Later I listened to the tape and could hear them praying, and then suddenly they all began to shout happily. What had happened to cause the sudden uproar of joy?

It was not what you might think. The sandwiches and Pepsi did not multiply. No, it was better than that. Suddenly a large cardboard box appeared on the grass directly in front of one of my friends. This frightened him so badly that he took a quick step backwards and he fell over another box that had appeared behind him. They opened the boxes to find prepackaged lunches in styrofoam containers. It was roast beef, mashed potatoes, gravy, and corn. My friends immediately looked around to see if anyone could have placed the boxes there, but there was no one in sight. They were standing on a level lawn hundreds of feet from any building. It was a miracle. There's just no other explanation.

The faith of those Mexicans was very inspiring. Probably not a single reader of this book would have prayed over some sandwiches and Pepsi asking God to multiply them. Maybe that's why we don't see as many miracles as we could. Maybe if we had the faith to always turn to Jesus as our first reaction when in time of need, we would see lots of miracles.

The Gift of Tongues

One last story from the Notre Dame conferences involves the gift of tongues. The Catholic Church teaches that speaking in tongues is one of the Gifts of the Holy Spirit, and that it is available for believers today as it has been since the day of Pentecost. But the gift of tongues has been widely misunderstood by many people both today and in the past. This is unfortunate because it really is a wonderful spiritual gift, which has been greatly neglected because of so much misinformation about it.

One of the best benefits of this gift is that it makes the power of God real. I know that I can't speak a foreign language, but when I'm speaking in tongues that's exactly what I'm doing. So it proves to me that God is at work in me. I've seen a similar effect in the lives of many others. It dramatically strengthens a person's faith in the power of God.

I could list many other benefits of this spiritual gift, but that's not the purpose of this book. I suggest that you get a copy of the book *Baptized in the Spirit* by Steve Clark. There you will find a good explanation of many spiritual gifts including the gift of tongues. Reading that little book could be a real eye-opener for you and lead you to a new life in the Spirit.

St. Paul teaches that when you speak in tongues you could be speaking in the language of men or angels. This was dramatically proven at a charismatic Mass at Notre Dame. Betty, my friend, and I were seated together at Mass with about ten thousand other people in Notre Dame's basketball arena. When it came time for Holy Communion, dozens of priests dispersed themselves throughout the arena to distribute Holy Communion to the faithful. As we approached in a line to receive Holy Communion I could hear Betty praying softly in tongues. This was not unusual and many others did the same.

When Mass was finished the stranger who was seated next to Betty and who had been in front of her in the

Communion line asked her this question, "Were you praying in tongues as you approached Communion?"

Betty recollected for a moment and answered that yes she had been speaking in tongues. He then informed her that he was from Scotland and that he knew a language called Gaelic. He told her that she had been speaking Gaelic and that he understood it.

She was flabbergasted, as she had no idea what language her gift of tongues was. Immediately she asked him, "What was I saying?"

He replied, "You repeated several times the same phrase. It was 'You are the Son of the Most High God'".

That incident was profound for two reasons. First, it proved the reality of the gift of tongues. It's not just some mumbo jumbo or meaningless babble. It's a real language and if someone who knew that language heard it, they would understand what was being said.

Secondly, and far more importantly, it proves the reality of the Holy Eucharist. The Catholic Church has always taught that the Holy Eucharist is the Body, Blood, Soul, and Divinity of Jesus Christ. It is really Christ present to us in a sacramental dimension. It doesn't just symbolize Jesus; it is Jesus. And that's what Betty was saying in tongues as she approached Holy Communion, "You are the Son of the Most High God." In the Spirit she was stating the awesome reality of the Holy Eucharist; it is the Son of God, Jesus Himself. St. Paul told us that when someone speaks in tongues, he utters mysteries in the Spirit. Well, there is no greater mystery than the Holy Eucharist. It is completely unexplainable how Jesus could give us his own Body and Blood and yet He did, and He still does today in every Mass throughout the world.

Everyday Signs

The prayer meetings and charismatic conferences were great, but God was also showing me His power everyday in the ordinary routine of life, where it matters most.

As I drove home from work one day I came upon a stranded car in the right lane of a very busy street in Sidney. The driver was trying his best to push the car and steer it at the same time. There was a gas station about two hundred yards ahead where he could get repairs, but it was slightly uphill all the way. I pulled my car off to the side and quickly jumped out to help. I pushed from behind the car with all my might and made some progress, but it was definitely an uphill battle. I didn't think we would make it, so I prayed like a guy who had seen miracles in the past. I prayed, "Dear Jesus, give me strength to push this car and help this guy out." I expected some sort of supernatural strength to flood my body, but just after I finished that prayer I heard a horn honk.

Behind me was a pick-up truck with a push board mounted to its front that was used to push cars. The chance of that truck being right there at that time is infinitesimally small. The truck driver motioned me out of the way and then easily pushed the stranded car to the gas station for help.

Walking back to my car I had to laugh at myself. I was praying for "super powers" when I should have been praying for a tow truck. God sent the help I needed but not in the way I expected. He does that a lot for all of us, but sometimes we're too stupid or stubborn to recognize it.

Fly Swatter

But sometimes you do need supernatural help because there's no natural help to be found. On one occasion I needed a fly swatter, but there wasn't one handy. I was sitting in the back row listening to a very important speaker who was giving our prayer group some advice on how we should organize ourselves so as to better serve the Lord. We were in the living room of the leader's home where I was sitting by a small table with a lamp on it. A large housefly was buzzing wildly around the room distracting many of the listeners. It really made me mad that this stupid fly was preventing a very important teaching from being effectively communicated.

Since I didn't have a fly swatter of any kind, I did what I thought was appropriate. I commanded the fly to die. Quietly, (I'm not that crazy!) I whispered, "In the name of Jesus, I command you to die." Instantly the fly fell from the air and landed dead on the table next to me. To kill a fly might not seem like much to you, but to me it was quite amazing.

Runaway Steers

One day some steers on our farm got loose through a hole in the fence. Chasing steers throughout the neighboring farms can quickly turn into a real nightmare. Dad drove down the road about half a mile or so in order to try to out-flank the steers. Standing at the roadside he could see the steers scattered across a large field, but he had no way of driving them back to the opening in the fence by himself. He said a quick prayer for help. A moment later a pick-up truck with a cap on its bed pulled over and stopped. The driver was a stranger in the area and asked Dad if there was something wrong. Dad explained the predicament he was facing with the out-of-control steers.

The man smiled and said, "I've got just what you need." He went to the back of his truck, opened the cap, and put down the tailgate. Out jumped two border collie dogs that were trained to herd cattle. He told Dad that all he had to do was tell him where he wanted the steers to go and the dogs would take care of the rest.

Dad couldn't believe his eyes. This was a perfect answer to his prayer. Quickly the dogs went about their work and were able to round up the steers and drive them right back through the opening in the fence from where they had escaped. All Dad had to do was walk across the field and watch the dogs and their handler work together to perfection. Soon the crisis was over.

Dad thanked the man as he loaded his dogs in the truck and got ready to leave. After he left Dad marveled at what had taken place. What were the chances of a complete stranger just happening to be passing by our farm with two cattle dogs at the exact moment that our steers had gotten loose! The odds had to be millions to one, and yet that's just what had happened. In Dad's mind there was no doubt that the hand of God was involved. Later Dad wondered if the stranger had actually been an angel. I guess we'll find out in Heaven.

The Lost Ring

There was another occasion when Dad had a dramatic answer to prayer. My brother John and his family always used to campout by the pond on the family farm each year on Memorial Day weekend. One year another family who were friends of theirs joined them. A week after the campout the father of the other family told John that he couldn't find his college ring and thought he might have lost it during the campout.

John was going to ask Dad if he would go out to the camping area and look for the ring, but he forgot to ask. It was over a month later when he remembered and finally told Dad about the lost ring. Talk about looking for a needle in a haystack! This was going to be nearly impossible to find. The grass had grown and hadn't been mowed, and there was no way of knowing where the tents had been located the previous month. The ring could have been anywhere in over an acre of long grass.

Dad was very busy the day John called but said he would take some time to look for the ring. Sometimes when Dad prayed he was pretty bold. He told the Lord that he was really busy and would appreciate it very much if the Lord would help him find the ring and *to find it quickly*. With that he drove out to the camping area. As he was getting out of the truck he saw something gleam in the bright sun in the grass about one hundred and fifty feet away. He walked over to the sparkling object and picked up the lost ring. He gave thanks and praise to God who had answered his prayer quickly.

St. Anthony

Over the years we have prayed to find many lost items. My family has always asked for the intercession of St. Anthony who is the patron saint of lost objects, and he has not let us down. We have been completely amazed time and again. St. Anthony has helped us so many times that it's become an automatic reflex for everyone in my family to turn to him for help when something has been lost.

My daughter Ruth prayed often to St. Anthony and urged others to do so as well. So much so, that the fiancée of one of her friends would make fun of her for her belief and devotion to St. Anthony. On one occasion Ruth went on a weekend canoeing and camping trip with about thirty young adults including her friend Mindy and Mindy's fiancé Chuck, who mocked Ruth for praying to St. Anthony for lost items.

Mindy, Chuck, and Ruth shared one canoe as they traveled down the river. When they arrived at the end of the trip they found out that the bus that was supposed to take them to the campsite had already left with everyone else aboard. So the three of them waited by the river thinking that sooner or later someone would realize that they were missing and come back to get them. They waited and waited. Two hours passed and there was no sign of help.

Finally Ruth said, "Let's pray to St. Anthony." Immediately Chuck began to mock her. He described himself as an atheist/agnostic who had no use for prayer to any God, much less a saint. Ruth was undaunted by his remarks and said she was going to pray to St. Anthony to help them. Chuck told Ruth that he would go to church with her the next Sunday if someone came to pick them up within fifteen minutes of her prayer. Ruth replied that it wouldn't take fifteen minutes but only five minutes for help to arrive. The challenge was made and the prayer was said. They checked their watches and waited.

Thirty seconds later a big Ford truck came over the hill and rumbled down the dirt path to pick them up and take them to the campsite. Ruthie danced a victory dance and thanked St. Anthony for his faithful intercession. Chuck stared in disbelief. His smug, atheistic, unbelieving attitude had just been shot down big time. There was nothing he could do about it except go to church with Ruth the next Sunday.

The Communion of Saints

Ruth's story brings up the whole concept of the Communion of Saints, which we profess every Sunday in the Nicene Creed. As Catholics we believe that all Christians, those on earth, in purgatory, and in heaven are connected spiritually in the one Mystical Body of Christ.

We are joined together by prayer, charity, and good works. We can and should pray for all the souls that are being purified in purgatory. Our prayers help them as they are being prepared for heaven. We look to the saints in heaven as our older brothers and sisters who have won the victory and who are now cheering us on as we run our race here on earth. They are in Heaven and in the direct presence of God. Their prayers on our behalf are very powerful for they have been perfected and they pray perfectly. We on earth are still struggling with our imperfections and so pray imperfectly.

I love that part of the Book of Job where God tells Job's three friends, who had spoken incorrectly about God in their ignorance of spiritual truths, that they should go to Job and have him pray for them. God told them that he would accept Job's prayer on their behalf because Job had been faithful and was righteous. It seems to me that if God accepts the prayers of a righteous person on earth for the needs of others, how much more will God accept the intercessory prayers offered to him by the saints in heaven.

I love all the saints, but of course, I have my favorites. Undoubtedly, the Blessed Virgin Mary should be everyone's favorite because she is the Queen of Heaven and the greatest of all the saints. She is the Immaculate One who did God's will perfectly on earth and in Heaven. Jesus gave her to all of us to be our spiritual mother when he spoke from the cross to St. John and said, *"Behold your mother."* St. John, the faithful disciple, represents the Church, all of us who are faithful disciples of Jesus. Just as John took Mary into his home, so also we should take Mary into our home, our heart, and allow her to live with us, teaching, protecting, providing, and leading us closer to Jesus.

I am constantly asking many of the saints in Heaven for their intercession. Over the years they have become my dearest friends, and it is such a comfort to be able to go to them in every need. Sometimes I imagine the Communion of Saints as a great and mighty river flowing to the sea. Each saint is one drop of water. I, too, am one drop and am being carried along by the force of billions upon billions of others who are ahead, behind, and all around me. I, too, am one tiny part of this huge current and affect others even as I am being carried along. It is gravity that pulls all of the water in the river to its destination, and it is the power of God who pulls all of us to Himself. This river image helps me to realize that my life is part of something a whole lot bigger than myself. When life seems overwhelming I know that I'll be carried along by billions of others who have gone before me and who will follow me. I know that I don't have to provide the power to keep moving forward, that power will be supplied by the lives of billions of others. I also know that life is moving; it's a continuum like the river with a beginning and an end, and that my life is a part of the grand journey that we are all making. My life is important and what I do with it is important because my life is intimately bound up with the life and destiny of billions of others who are all a part of the great river. The doctrine of the Communion of Saints is a reality to me. It's a reality that allows me to be carried along by others, but at the same time know that I am an important part of the whole and that I will play my part in bringing others to Christ. I eagerly look forward to that day when I will praise God in Heaven in the company of the Blessed Virgin Mary, all the angels, St. Joseph, St. Anthony, St. Bernadette, St. Isaac Jogues, St. Therese, St. Francis of Assisi, St. Francis De Sales, St. Joan of Arc, St. Remy, St. Vincent Ferrer, St. Anne, and all of the saints who have been my dearest companions here on earth.

California Trip

In the summer of 1976 I went on a road trip vacation with two of my good friends, Steve and Ron. We drove my car from Ohio to California and back over a three-week period of time. We were sightseers and did we ever get our fill. We saw Mt. Rushmore, Lake Tahoe, the desert, San Francisco, the Fresno Valley, the giant sequoia trees, Los Angeles, Las Vegas, the Grand Canyon, the Rocky Mountains, the Air Force Academy, the wheat fields of Kansas, the Arch of St. Louis, and many more things too numerous to mention.

As a Christian I try to be a Good Samaritan to people in need along the highway. I've picked up many hitchhikers and stopped to help people with broken down vehicles from time to time. Before we left home for our road trip I told God that I didn't think I would be able to help all the people we might come across in need and still be able to get our trip completed in three weeks. But I didn't want to be completely selfish and not help anyone, so I told the Lord that He could show me the person that He wanted me to help and I would do it.

So I let my mind go blank like a television screen and after a few moments a picture appeared in my mind. It was a woman who was hitchhiking, and I could see her clearly. I told the Lord that when I saw her I would give her a ride.

A few days into our trip I saw that very woman trying to hitch a ride. I was driving on an interstate highway in Salt Lake City, Utah, and the traffic was very heavy and fast. I was about three lanes from the right side of the road and there was no way for me to get through all of the traffic to get to the side of the road to pick her up. By the time I did get over to the right lane, I was several miles past her so I just kept on going.

I felt really bad because God had shown me that woman in my mind, and I had promised God I would help her. Now I had failed, but I told God that it wasn't my fault. The traffic had prevented me from getting to her. That evening I prayed again and asked the Lord to show me another person that He wanted me to help. This time a picture appeared in my mind of a young man with his suitcase, standing beneath an overpass on a rather sharp curve.

Two days later we were about to cross the desert, and I entered the entrance ramp to the interstate. As I rounded the curve, there he was, the young man with the suitcase. I could have picked him up very easily, but I didn't. I just passed him by.

Why didn't I pick him up? Several thoughts raced instantly through my mind when I saw him. We were just entering the desert, and there were big flashing signs saying that there were no exits for the next two hundred miles. I knew that if I gave him a ride he would be in our car for at least several hours and didn't know if Steve and Ron would like that very much. I didn't want to take the chance of upsetting my buddies so I just passed him by.

I felt absolutely terrible as I drove through that desert. My mind was filled with regret, and I felt about as desolate as the barren landscape that stretched as far as I could see. At that point I had not yet told Steve and Ron about my deal with God to help someone on our trip and how He had shown me two people, both of whom I had failed to help. After several hours of mental misery, I told them all about what had happened. I also decided that if God would forgive me for passing up the young man and give me another chance that I was going to help the person no matter what they might think. They had no resistance to my plan at all and wondered why I had thought there would be a problem.

As I prayed that evening, I asked God to give me another chance and He did. He showed me in my mind a red-haired young man with a green knapsack on his back standing by a long gently curving guardrail in the median of an interstate. I told Steve and Ron the description of the man. As we drove, we were on the lookout for him.

It was fifteen days later, and we were on our last day of our trip when I spotted him on Interstate 70 as we approached the Gateway to the West Arch in St. Louis. But once again the traffic was thick and I was in the wrong lane. It was impossible to get to him so I told Steve and Ron that I would drop them off at the Arch,

which was a few miles ahead, and then I would go back
to pick him up.

I made sure I drove back far enough and then I
crossed over the interstate highway and started heading
east again. I got into the left lane and approached the
place where he had been earlier. Much to my surprise he
was gone! It had only taken me about ten minutes to get
back to where he had been, but he was gone! I didn't
feel bad this time because I had done all I could to help
him, but it was out of my control. As I drove down the
highway I was actually a little irritated. I told God that I
didn't understand what He was doing with me. At that
moment God spoke to me very clearly and said, "I just
wanted to see if you would do it." That was all that
needed to be said. I instantly understood.

God doesn't really need me or anyone or anything
else in the universe. God is completely self-sufficient and
He is completely happy and fulfilled in Himself. Of His
own free will He chose to create everything and everyone to share His goodness. He didn't need to create; He
just chose to do it.

And God didn't need me to pick up that hitchhiker.
He could have provided transportation for that man in a
thousand different ways. So what am I saying? Is life just
a big stupid game that God plays with us? No, not at all.

Life is all about relationships. Really. That's what it all
comes down to in the end. Life is about our relationship
with God, and consequently, our relationship with our
neighbor. Eventually the universe and everything in it will
cease to exist, but that's not true of God or of us. We, like
God, are immortal spirits and will live forever. The ques-

tion that this life answers is what will our eternal relationship be with God. Will it be a relationship of love or hate, of obedience or rebellion? However that question is answered in this life determines our eternal destiny.

By the way, it's an essay question (sorry, you multiple-choice or matching fans). It's an essay that we write each day of our life with every thought, word, and deed we perform. That day on Interstate 70, I was answering a very small part of my essay question. When I said yes to God by trying to pick up the hitchhiker, there was no need for anything else. God had gotten the answer He wanted - my obedience, my yes, and my love. That's the one thing that is truly mine to give to God - my yes, my love. My ability to love God is a gift from Him in the first place. After all, He created me with a free will and without it I could not love or hate, obey or disobey.

But I do have a free will, and God will not force me to obey Him or to love Him. I can choose and so can you, my Friend. I have chosen Jesus and want to be in a loving relationship with Him forever. What will your decision be? Remember, that in the end, all that remains is relationships. Someday either Jesus or Satan will reach out and embrace you and say, "*Mine!*"

Square Dance

In Genesis, chapter twenty-four, Abraham's servant asked God for a sign to guide him in doing his master's will, and God gave him the sign he asked for. Will God do the same for us today?

First of all, you must ask for a specific sign, something somewhat out of the ordinary. Abraham's servant asked God for a woman who would offer to water his camels. It would certainly be unusual for a stranger to undertake the considerable amount of work involved in watering ten camels, especially when Abraham's servant had only asked the woman for a drink of water for himself.

Secondly, you must be totally willing to accept God's will in the matter you are asking about. This only makes sense. After all, if you've already made up your mind about what you are going to do, why ask God for a sign to "guide" you? God is not in for playing mind games. (If He were, we would all be in for big trouble!) If you're not open to God's will in the matter at hand, don't expect God to give you a sign – He won't! But if your will is open to His, go ahead and ask and expect God to answer.

About two years after my conversion, I was invited to the wedding of two of my college friends. The only problem was that I was also scheduled to be on a weekend retreat that same Saturday. I hated to leave the retreat, but I decided it was important that I attend the reception dinner. Catholic weddings in my rural area are loads of fun. After the wedding Mass, hundreds of people are invited to an evening reception filled with good food, drink, and dancing. A typical 22-year old man like me would bring his girlfriend as a date to enjoy the celebration. But I didn't have a date. In fact, I had had only two dates in the previous two years. During my four years of college, I had dated more than two-dozen different girls.

But after my conversion, I changed my standards about whom I would date. I would only go out with someone who shared my religious beliefs, and I had not found many girls who answered that description.

As I drove the fifteen miles from the retreat house to the wedding reception, I was feeling somewhat uncomfortable about not having a date. I told God how I was feeling, and I asked God a question. "Do you care about the fact that I don't have a date?" It was important to me to know that God cared about me in every way. Of course, intellectually and theologically I believed that God was all knowing and all loving, and I expressed that belief to God in prayer as I drove down the rural highway. But I felt it would be nice if God would give me a sign to show me that He cared about me and my situation. I told God that I would believe in Him and love Him just the same if He decided not to send me a sign, but if He wanted to do a favor for me, it would sure make my day if He sent me a sign.

"What sign should I ask for?" I thought to myself. I have always enjoyed the square dancing at weddings, and if I had a date I would surely like to square dance with her. So that's what I asked for. I prayed, "Lord, have a girl ask me to square dance with her." That might not seem unusual today, but in 1977 it was very unusual for a girl to ask a boy to dance. It was certainly something that had never happened to me. As I drove along I thought that maybe I might be "drafted" into dancing at the last moment to fill out the four couples needed for square dancing. I had seen that happen many times before. So I told the Lord, "Please have the girl ask me to dance at least a half hour before the dance so I'll know it's You."

Also, I wanted to get back to the retreat as soon as I could so I didn't want to spend the whole evening waiting for the sign to occur. So I told the Lord to have the girl ask me to dance at least half an hour before the very first square dance of the evening.

Well, since I was asking, I thought that I might as well ask for a pretty girl. So I did. I told the Lord to make this girl the prettiest girl at the reception and to allow us to have a great time together.

There was only one more thing that I requested. I asked the Lord that in some way it would be made known to me that my friends who were getting married had appreciated the fact that I had attended the wedding under some inconvenient and uncomfortable circumstances.

I arrived at the reception and began to wait for the sign that only God and I knew about. I socialized with friends and had a delicious dinner buffet. Just after finishing my dessert, a beautiful blonde-haired woman came over to my table, looked me right in the eye, and said, "You just have to square dance with me the very first square dance!" I could hardly believe it! It was just as I had prayed for! The first square dance was an hour away, and she was definitely a pretty girl. We had known each other in college several years before, and she knew I could square dance. She had come to the reception with a date, but he didn't know how to square dance, so she asked me.

I quickly accepted her invitation to dance and about an hour later we danced up a storm and had a really good time. I enjoyed it thoroughly! (Actually, the next week some of the guys asked me who the beautiful girl was and how I got to dance with her. I told them that you just have to have the right "connections.")

But it wasn't the dancing that was the cause of my joy. No, my heart was flooded that evening with a joy that came straight from God. I knew that God had sent me a sign and that He cared about me. I knew that God had heard my prayer. I felt really close to God and that is a great feeling.

It was early in the evening when I had finished my square dancing. I said my farewell to friends and was about to leave the reception to go back to the retreat. As I walked toward the exit, I thought to myself, "Lord, you did really well. You answered all of my conditions except the one about feeling appreciated for attending the wedding, but that's okay." As my hand touched the door, I heard my name being called by a female voice. I turned to see the maid-of-honor hurrying towards me. She said, "Henry, I'm so glad I caught you before you left. I just wanted to say how much we appreciated you making the effort to come to the wedding. It just wouldn't have been the same if you hadn't been here."

As I walked across the parking lot to my car, I was filled with happiness. God had showed me that He doesn't miss the slightest detail and that He knows and cares about every part of my life. Knowing God in this personal way is life-changing. It allows a person to truly follow God's will in every circumstance and know that

God will be right there with you every step of the way. Such knowledge makes truly great things possible.

I have told this story many times to freshman students in my religion class. The reactions vary – some don't believe it ever happened, some believe that it happened to me but wouldn't happen to them, and others want to try praying like this themselves. Many times students return to class the next day and have their own sign story to tell.

One boy shared his story with me after class. The school homecoming dance was approaching. He wanted to ask a certain girl, but was afraid she would say no. So he asked God for a sign. If it happened, he would ask the girl. If it didn't happen, he wouldn't. He told the Lord, "Have this girl offer me a piece of gum." She had never done this before, and he thought it would be quite unusual if it occurred. Before homeroom the next day the students were standing in the hall by their lockers. The girl walked down the hall and came up to this boy and offered him a piece of gum. He was amazed! As he told me the story I could see that what was really important was the fact that God had heard his prayer and had communicated back to him. He knew that he could now talk with God, and he knew it with his whole heart. I don't remember if the girl went to the dance with him or not. That's not important. What is important is that for the rest of his life that boy will know that God hears every word he prays.

How about you, my Friend? Do you really know that God hears your prayers and cares about you? Wouldn't you love to have God communicate with you? It probably won't happen until you give God a chance. So why not take time right now and pray to God for a sign concerning something that's important to you. Make sure you follow the conditions I stated above. When God answers your prayer be sure to thank Him and then write to me and tell me your story. I'd love to read it!

Jane's Conversion

One night I had a dream from God. I realize that we all dream in our sleep and that sometimes those dreams are extremely vivid and real to us, but I'm talking about a whole different level of dreaming. I can't adequately explain the experience other than to say that if you ever have a dream from God, you'll know it. I have had two such dreams, and both have produced dramatic results.

The dream I had was very simple. In the dream, Jane, a former classmate of mine, appeared hovering over my bed as if she were an angel looking down upon me as I lay in bed. I could tell that it was her because the face was clear but the rest of her body was some sort of bright light. She spoke and said, "God is love." That was all she said, but it was an overpowering experience.

I awoke in an agitated state. The dream dominated my thoughts, although I had no idea what might have been the purpose of the dream. Normally a person soon forgets what they dreamed the night before but that was not the case with this dream. Everyday for the next month that dream would come back to my mind, and I just couldn't forget it. I wondered why this was happening and finally decided that I should call Jane and tell her about my dream.

Jane and I had been good friends throughout grade school and high school, but I hadn't seen her more than a couple of times in the four years since our graduation. She lived in Dayton, Ohio, and worked in the office of a utility company. I found her phone number and began to dial it, but I stopped halfway through it.

I thought to myself that what I was doing was going to seem very ridiculous. I was going to tell someone I hadn't seen in years that they appeared as an angel to me in a dream and said, "God is love," and I didn't even know why I should tell her about it. I hung up the phone and walked away telling myself to forget about it. But I couldn't. Everyday at some point the thought would arise in my mind that I should tell Jane about the dream.

There was a wedding in Russia that I was invited to attend and thought that Jane was probably invited also. I called her and asked her if she was going. She said yes, and since neither of us had a date we decided to go together. I told her that I had something that I wanted to tell her, but I wanted to talk to her about it in person.

When I picked her up to go to the wedding reception she immediately questioned me about what it was that I wanted to tell her. I described the dream and its message and how it had stayed with me. She didn't know anything about my conversion, so I took the opportunity to explain all the great things that had happened to me.

At first she was somewhat skeptical and privately questioned my friend, Roger, who was also at the reception, if this whole story was some kind of elaborate joke or prank that I was trying to play upon her. Roger assured her that it was no joke and that he had also experienced the Baptism in the Holy Spirit which had become the transforming event of his life.

After that corroboration from Roger, Jane began to listen very intently as I explained to her the new life in the Spirit. We spoke together for the next six hours, and I opened up a whole new spiritual world for her consideration. It felt great to share my faith with an old friend.

A couple of weeks later I called her on the phone to see what she thought about our spiritual conversation. She told me that all she could think about since that day was that she had to go to Confession and seek God's forgiveness. What a perfect result! Repentance is the first step we take in following Jesus. Like the prodigal son, when someone decides to return home and to ask forgiveness for their sins, that's when God our Father can embrace us and hold us close to Himself. Then He showers us with gifts, and we rejoice together.

I told her to go to Confession and to really confess with all of her heart. I told her to make a clean sweep of her entire life and to receive the Lord's mercy into her heart. After her confession, I would visit her and pray with her for the Baptism in the Holy Spirit. That was the plan, and that's what we did. After she made a good general confession of her life, I came to pray with her. We prayed that the Holy Spirit would fill her with His presence and give her His gifts. As we prayed she received the gift of tongues and was filled with the joy and the peace of the Lord. We thanked God for His goodness and mercy that He had bestowed upon both of us. Since that day Jane has been on fire for the Lord and has brought the message of Christ to many, many people. What started as a dream has borne a lot of good fruit.

Heavenly Scent

I was experiencing tremendous spiritual phenomena in the Catholic Charismatic Renewal along with some of my family and friends. My Dad had experienced the Baptism in the Holy Spirit, but my Mom hadn't. I talked to her about my conversion and the new life in the Spirit and all of the exciting spiritual gifts that I had seen operating in the lives of many people. Mom was not receptive at all to what I was saying. She had a spiritual life of her own, which I would describe as classic Catholicism. Everyday she prayed the Rosary. She read traditional prayers from her prayer book, read from the lives of the saints, and prayed privately. Sunday Mass, litanies, and novenas were staples in her spiritual diet. When I would tell her about spiritual gifts would tell me that she didn't understand them and she was just going to stick to her own spirituality because she was happy with it and felt safe and secure.

While she was feeling good about her spirituality, I wasn't. It concerned me. I even started to worry about her salvation because I was so enthusiastic about my new life in the Spirit that I just couldn't imagine that anyone else wouldn't want to experience it also. I viewed her traditional Catholic spirituality as pretty "dead" and I wanted to make sure that my Mom, whom I loved very much, was really on her way to Heaven. So I began to pray for my Mom a lot. I prayed that she would give her life to Christ and be filled with the Holy Spirit in the same way that had changed my life and many others so dramatically.

I was making a classic mistake at that time and was completely unaware of it. I was thinking that my experience of God was the experience that everyone should have. In my spiritual immaturity I didn't realize that God works in various ways in people's lives. God was about to teach me this valuable lesson.

I went to a charismatic retreat at Maria Stein Retreat Center which wasn't far from where I lived. During some free time I walked over to the relic chapel which housed hundreds of relics of saints from all over the world and from every century. I think it is one of the largest collection of relics in North America and is certainly a very sacred place. While at the relic chapel my mother was very much on my mind, and I prayed fervently for her salvation which I had doubts about because of her rejection of the charismatic renewal.

When I finished praying I walked across the beautiful grounds surrounding the main retreat house. As I walked I came upon a beautiful honeysuckle bush that was in full bloom. I stopped and pulled a branch filled with blooms to my face and smelled the wonderful fragrance of the flowers.

At that exact moment God spoke to me in an unmistakable fashion and said, "***Your mother smells the same way to me.***"

It was so unexpected and yet so clear what God had said to me. I was overwhelmed and thrilled at the same

time. I can't explain how happy those words made me
feel at that moment. Any and all doubts about my Mother's holiness or salvation were completely removed and
never returned. The smell of the flowers was heavenly
and if that represented my Mother's status with God, then
I was certain that she was in very good standing with the
Lord.

I didn't realize at that time that my Mother's classic
Catholic spirituality would become my own spirituality in
due time. Her spirituality was actually more mature and
stable than my own charismatic spirituality. Don't get me
wrong. I'm very grateful for all the spiritual gifts that I've
experienced in the charismatic renewal and those gifts
have produced a lot of good fruit. But spiritual gifts are
not the end of the road. They're just the beginning. All
spiritual gifts should lead us into a deeper relationship
with Jesus and the Church.

Over the years I've seen some people who were very
charismatic actually lose their faith and stray away from
the Catholic Church because they thought that they knew
more than the Church. They trusted in their own opinion
more than in the teaching of the Magisterium of the
Church. That is a huge mistake, which leads to spiritual
ruin.

My own spirituality was very charismatic for about
twelve years, and then I became much more Marian. As
my devotion to Mary increased I became more traditionally Catholic. Today I like to classify myself as an extrem-
ist – I'm in the extreme center of the Catholic Church. I'm
not on the right wing or the left wing; I'm in the center
of the flock. The sheep that get eaten by the wolf are the

ones on the edge of the flock or those that have strayed from the flock completely. I don't want to be eaten by the wolf so I try to stay right in the middle of the flock, right by the shepherd where there is safety. For me that means that I accept and follow all the teachings of the Catholic Church wholeheartedly. Not only do I accept the teachings of the Pope, my shepherd, I rejoice in the fact that God has given me and the Church an infallible guide to lead us in faith and morality here on earth. It is such a blessing to know that I don't have to figure out everything myself, but that I can look to the Church for true guidance.

Today my spirituality is very similar to what my Mother's was thirty years ago. Daily Mass, daily Rosary and private prayer are the foundation. I do a lot of spiritual reading, listen to tapes, wear my scapular, practice devotion to the Sacred Heart of Jesus and the Immaculate Heart of Mary, pray the Divine Mercy Chaplet, participate in Eucharistic adoration and go to confession bi-weekly. I still pray in tongues everyday and look for the power of the Holy Spirit to be active in my life, but I'm much less charismatic today and much more traditionally Catholic. I believe this transition from charismatic to classic Catholicism has been the work of the Holy Spirit in my life and is a transition that has been mirrored around the world in the lives of millions of other charismatic Catholics.

It's embarrassing for me to admit that I was once concerned about my Mother's salvation and thought her spirituality was "dead," when in actuality she was far more spiritually advanced than me. But thankfully God taught me and led me into a deeper spirituality that bears even more good fruit. Hopefully, I can advance spiritually to the point that my fragrance will be as wonderful as that of my mother.

Exorcisms

Fr. Jim was the pastor of Holy Angels Parish and was a good friend of mine. On one occasion he had a family who came to him for help in stopping the strange occurrences that were happening in their home. The middle-aged parents lived with their two adult sons in a small house situated in the peaceful countryside, but inside the house it was anything but peaceful. Day after day they heard someone walking in the upstairs rooms where the boys slept. The sounds of footsteps were unmistakable, but there wasn't anyone up there. There were other unexplainable noises coming from upstairs, and the family was understandably agitated. One evening as they were watching television, a woman appeared in the room. She seemed to be about sixty years old with gray hair and dressed in black. She didn't speak at all but simply walked across the room and through the wall into the kitchen. After crossing the kitchen she passed through the exterior wall to the yard where she disappeared. This really freaked them out and they turned to Fr. Jim for help. Fr. Jim gave them a bottle of holy water and told them to sprinkle it throughout their house and to pray for God's protection from anything evil. When they tried to go upstairs to sprinkle the holy water, the family met an invisible resistance. They were frozen in place on the stairs and could not move forward. After some minutes they managed to back down the stairs and close the door.

It was springtime and the air was cool, but inside the house the family was freezing. They turned the furnace on high and burned a kerosene heater until the thermometer on the wall registered over 100 degrees, but they were still freezing while wearing their winter coats inside the house. What happened next really pushed them over the edge. The elderly woman appeared again. This time she appeared in the parents' bedroom while they were sleeping and began to choke the husband. As he struggled to fight against her, she suddenly disappeared. That was it! They couldn't take it anymore. The family moved to the Holiday Inn and once again asked Fr. Jim for help. He told them he would try.

Fr. Jim asked me and four other prayer group members to help him do an exorcism upon the house. The only time we could all go together to the house was after the Tuesday evening prayer meeting, so that's what we planned to do. We prepared as best we could with prayer and fasting. Fr. Jim brought the Holy Eucharist with him in a golden container. Before we left, we prayed in church and asked God for a Scripture passage. What we received was Psalm 68, "*God rises up and scatters His enemies. Those who hate Him run away in defeat. As smoke is blown away, so He drives them off.*" With that encouraging word, we left.

We had planned to meet the family at 10:30 p.m. They arrived a few minutes before us and were waiting at the back porch of the house. As the six of us arrived in Fr. Jim's car, a chaotic sound could be heard. It was as if fifty people were running through the house and yelling loudly. In a moment the stampede was over. Everything was quiet. It's my opinion that the evil spirits sensed the arrival of Jesus in the Holy Eucharist and fled in terror.

We all entered the house and met no resistance at all. We went through every room in the house, and Fr. Jim sprinkled holy water and led prayers. When we had finished we sat in the living room for a while and spoke with the family. With our encouragement they decided to stay in their home. Nothing abnormal occurred until two weeks later.

In the detached garage, one of the boys was changing the oil in his car when he saw something dreadfully frightful. As he slid from under the car to reach for a wrench, he caught sight of a demon sitting in the corner of the garage. He described it as a dark, hideous creature unlike anything he had ever seen. It was about two feet tall with red eyes staring at him. He was terrified and ran out of the garage as fast as he could.

Once again the family called Fr. Jim for help. We followed the same procedure as we had done two weeks before only this time it was the garage that was exorcised. We hadn't thought of doing the garage the first time because the family hadn't reported anything happening there and it wasn't part of the house.

Thankfully, the second exorcism finished the job, and the family was never bothered again. Some people today don't believe in the existence of evil spirits. I think that's a very stupid point of view. Others go to the other extreme and see demons behind every difficulty in life.

That, too, is very stupid and often just a means of avoiding personal responsibility for their own sinfulness.

The Church teaches that demons are fallen angels. God created them as good angels, but they failed the test of loving God definitively and have been cast out of God's presence. They hate God and hate man who's made in God's image. They war against mankind and attempt to bring people to damnation along with themselves. We are all involved in a war for our souls. The Devil is a liar, and one of his best lies is that he doesn't exist. When people believe that lie they leave themselves wide open to the attacks of the Devil.

Our best defense against the evil spirits is to live lives of holiness. When we are filled with God's grace and His Holy Spirit, the Devil can't get a foothold in our life. I believe in using every means available to live a holy life. Our greatest weapons are the Sacraments of the Church, especially Holy Eucharist and Confession. But don't neglect sacramentals such as holy water, the Rosary, and the Brown Scapular. These sacramentals are very helpful to us in pursuing holiness and warding off evil spirits.

I'll tell you one more story of an encounter with the Devil. It was a beautiful summer day when I met Stan. It was noon when I met him on the sidewalk as I was going home to lunch. He said he would give me a dollar if I would give him a ride to the Tack Room, a local bar about a mile away. I told him to keep his money and that I'd be glad to give him a ride. As he got into my car he proudly announced that it was his thirtieth birthday and that he was going to celebrate by getting drunk. I congratulated him on his birthday, but I tried to convince him not to get drunk.

I knew he would only be in my car a couple of minutes so I acted quickly and asked him "Do you love Jesus?" He said that he used to love Jesus but had become a backslider and an alcoholic. I told him that I used to get drunk all the time but Jesus had set me free.

He broke down immediately and began to pour out his troubles to me. He told me how drinking was ruining his life. He said that his wife was divorcing him and taking their three little children because of his drinking.

I assured him that Jesus could set him free from alcohol and asked him if that was what he wanted. He said, "That would be great, but not today. Today's my birthday and I'm going to get drunk."

By this time we had arrived at the bar's parking lot, and we were just sitting and talking. For quite a while I tried to convince him not to put off the decision to quit drinking. I quoted the Scripture that says, "*Today is the day of salvation,*" and explained to him that the more you say no to God's grace, the harder it becomes to say yes to God. My giving him a ride was God's way of reaching out to him yet again, and he shouldn't push the hand of God away. Even with all of my urgings, he was not moved to abandon his plan for that day.

Finally, I asked if I could pray over him. He said that it would be okay. I laid a hand upon his shoulder and began to pray that the Holy Spirit would soften his heart and help him turn away from drinking. I prayed that the precious blood of Jesus would cover him and cleanse him from all evil. At the mention of the precious blood of

Jesus, Stan suddenly spoke in a voice that sounded like it came straight from hell. A deep, guttural, unearthly voice said, "**I'm not ready to leave yet.**"

Visibly shaken, Stan asked, "Where did that voice come from?"

I replied, "It came from your mouth."

Instantly, I knew that Stan's drinking problem also had a demonic facet to it. I didn't think it was wise to try to do an impromptu exorcism in the front seat of my compact car. I thought it would be best if Stan went to see Fr. Jim at Holy Angels and allow him to deal with this problem. I asked Stan if he knew Fr. Jim and was surprised to hear that he was familiar with him even though Stan was not a Catholic. I gave him Fr. Jim's phone number and told him to set up an appointment to see him and to tell him what had happened in the car. He said he would, but I don't know if he ever did. The last I saw of Stan, he was walking into the bar to get drunk. I was unable to stop him.

To hear the voice of a demon speaking through a man from two feet away is a frightening experience and something I hope I never hear again. I really don't like to be involved in things that deal with evil spirits because it can be so frightening. We should all be very thankful that the Catholic Church provides brave Catholic priests to do exorcisms that sometimes are necessary.

My Friend, the Devil is real. He is your enemy who wants to drag you to Hell for all eternity. He will take advantage of any opening you give him through sinning in any way. Don't live in sin! If you fall into mortal sin of any kind you should make an act of contrition and tell

God you are sorry right away. Then you must make up your mind to go to Confession the first opportunity that's available to you so that you can receive the Lord's forgiveness and be reconciled with God and the Church. Some people make the terrible mistake of living in mortal sin for long periods of time. That is extremely dangerous!

If you die in mortal sin you will be lost to Hell forever. Satan will have you for all eternity and the torture you will suffer is beyond anything you can imagine. Jesus compared the pain of Hell to an unquenchable fire, and of course the symbol never lives up to the reality. How would you feel if you were covered with gasoline and then set on fire? Hell is worse than that and lasts forever!

When someone lives in mortal sin for long periods of time they become spiritually numb or desensitized. In time their conscience becomes warped, and they no longer see sin as the evil it is. Eventually their conscience will die, and they will be able to commit the most horrible sins, without any remorse. Such a person may even start to think that evil is actually good. Abortionists who march down the street demanding that abortion remain legal would fit into this category. Such people call evil "good" because their "light" is actually darkness. Jesus warned us in the Gospel not to let our light be darkness.

This is what living in sin does to a person, and I don't want that to happen to you, my Friend. If you fall into sin through weakness, run to Jesus who will forgive you and take you back seven times a day if necessary. Constantly turn to Jesus and He will strengthen you to live in His grace where you will be safe from the Evil One.

Part V
The Mustard Seed

Priesthood or Marriage

The years following my conversion were filled with many spiritual activities. I was on fire for the Lord and was trying to serve Him in every way I could. I guess it was only natural that I should give some consideration to the thought of becoming a priest. In fact, I gave it a lot of consideration. I went on a vocation retreat sponsored by the Archdiocese of Cincinnati, the diocese in which I live. I met with Fr. Jim at Holy Angels Parish on a regular basis to talk with him and to discern my vocation.

This discernment process weighed heavily on my mind because it's a very big decision. To become a Catholic priest is the highest calling that a Catholic man can aspire to. A priest acts *In Persona Christi* (in the person of Christ) when he administers the Sacraments. A priest has the power to forgive sins and to change the bread and wine into the Body and Blood of Christ. The whole life of a priest involves awesome powers and responsibilities. These are extremely weighty matters for a young man in his early twenties to consider.

Choosing priesthood is also a lifelong choice. When a man becomes a priest he is consecrated as a priest forever and will have to fulfill his duties as a priest for the rest of his life. There's also celibacy to consider. A priest is not allowed to marry. By remaining single he can give himself totally to the service of God and the Church. He becomes a constant reminder to all of the faithful that the Kingdom of God is coming, where there will be no marriage but Christ will unite everyone to Himself. I didn't know if I could handle celibacy. I had always thought that someday I would get married and have a family, but maybe God was calling me to abandon those ideas and embrace celibacy.

After a year of careful prayer and consideration of all the issues involved, I decided to apply to the seminary in Cincinnati. I went through the various testing procedures and interviews and received word in June that I had been accepted and would start classes in the fall of 1977. For the next two months I had no peace about this decision. For some reason it just didn't seem to me that I should go to the seminary. Maybe it was just my natural human fears or maybe it was the action of the Holy Spirit, but something had me very agitated about the situation so I decided to inform the seminary that I wouldn't be attending classes in the fall. My mother was very disappointed because she had always wanted one of her eight sons to become a priest, and as the youngest, I was her last hope. Although she was disappointed, I felt a great sense of relief and my peace returned. But the thought of priesthood hadn't been erased completely and still remained in the back of my mind.

That fall I met the girl that I would eventually marry, but not without a lot of gut-wrenching soul searching. I was greeting people at the door of the Holy Angels prayer meeting when I met Ann Fisher. She was a beautiful and cheerful young woman who immediately caught my attention. Some of her friends at work had told her about the prayer group, and she had decided to check it out herself.

It just happened that I was scheduled to give a teaching that night, and I spoke to the group on a spiritual topic for about forty-five minutes. After we were married, Ann revealed to me that as she listened to me speak that evening she knew that she was going to marry me. We had only met for a moment and said hello, but she already knew. It's amazing how sometimes the Lord reveals things to one person but not to another. I certainly didn't have any such revelation and, in fact, the decision to get married was the toughest decision I've ever had to struggle through.

The reason it was so difficult was because I was attracted to both priesthood and marriage, and I didn't know which one was God's will for me. As the weeks passed, Ann and I saw each other at the prayer meetings and got to know each other a little. We began to do some social things together with a group of other young adults who also attended the prayer meetings. We worked with others to organize and start a Christian coffeehouse where single Christians could get together on the weekends to socialize.

For two and a half years I had been following the good advice of Pastor Peter who had drawn the triangle on the blackboard and said that everyone should seek to do God's will and allow God to bring your spouse to you. It seemed to me that Ann might be the person that

God had brought into my life as I was seeking to serve Him. On the tenth of December we had our first date.

It was a Saturday afternoon, and we went to a local Christmas tree dealer and to buy a tree for Ann's apartment. We took it home and spent the rest of the day decorating it with all of the handmade ornaments that Ann had made over the years. We talked and talked that day. The depth of our communication was simply amazing. Ann really started it when she confessed all the worst sins of her life to me and then said that if I couldn't deal with her past, there would be no sense in having a second date. I told her that if God had forgiven her, who was I to pass any kind of judgment upon her. Then I confessed the sins of my terrible life to her, and she accepted me also. That set the pattern for a tremendous amount of in-depth communication that would occur almost daily (we had apartments across the street from each other) for the next several months. By February we were discussing the possibility of marriage.

We were in complete agreement on the Catholic faith and moral issues like contraception and divorce. We both accepted the Catholic Church's teaching on every topic, including the Church's view of married life and sexuality. We were in agreement on the roles of husband and wife and how we should approach our careers. We were in love with each other and the thought of marriage was very appealing to us. There was only one problem – maybe God wanted me to be a priest.

I couldn't shake the thought from my mind that maybe it was God's will that I become a priest. This dilemma became the central topic of our conversation each day, and it was driving me crazy.

Ann was great. She always said that if God wanted me to be a priest then that's what I should do. She never tried to talk me away from the priesthood. Even though she wanted to marry me, she wanted to do God's will more than her own. That's the perfect attitude that we should all try to have in every situation. It was Jesus' attitude when He said, *"Father, if there is any way possible, let this cup pass away from Me. Yet not My will but Thy will be done."* It was Mary's attitude when she said, *"I am the handmaid of the Lord. Let it be done unto me according to Your word."*

Ann had demonstrated her complete devotion to Christ before we had ever met each other. She had been engaged to marry a local man named Fred. He was a Lutheran who was divorced from his wife when he met and dated Ann. They had gone to see Fr. Jim at Holy Angels Parish to make wedding arrangements. When Fr. Jim learned that Fred had been previously married, he explained that Fred would have to apply for an annulment and that it would have to be approved by the Archdiocese before they could enter into a valid marriage. So the annulment paperwork was filed, and they waited for a reply from the Archdiocese. After several months Fr. Jim called them to a meeting at the rectory. At this meeting he told Fred and Ann that they could not be married in the Catholic Church because the Church had determined that Fred's marriage was valid and that in the eyes of God he was still married to the woman he had divorced. This was not the result that they had expected, but there wasn't anything they could do about it. They said goodbye to Fr. Jim and left the rectory.

On the sidewalk outside the rectory Ann told Fred that since the Church had determined that he was a married man, they would no longer be able to date and their relationship was over. She took off the engagement ring and gave it back to him, said her goodbye, and went home. It was over just like that.

I was so impressed by Ann's character. She had obeyed the Church quickly and without complaint. She truly believed that the Church was speaking for Christ in this matter and didn't hesitate to obey its ruling. There are many cafeteria Catholics who would not have acted the way she did. They would have simply gone somewhere else and gotten married without church approval and rationalized their actions in their own minds. But Ann was not a cafeteria Catholic; she was a truly faithful Catholic and that made her extremely desirable to me.

I continued to struggle daily with trying to discern God's will for my life. I prayed as fervently and earnestly as I have ever prayed in my life asking God to reveal His will in the matter and to guide me to the correct decision. Yet no matter how hard I prayed, I didn't seem to get an answer. Eventually a decision needed to be made so Ann and I decided on a course of action.

We decided that it was our intention to marry but we wanted to make sure that it was God's will. So we prayed and asked God to give us a sign that would confirm our decision. We decided that we wouldn't tell anyone or make any marriage plans until we received a sign from God. After only a few days of praying, we got an answer.

I received a phone call from Jane who was an old classmate of mine and whom I had led to the Lord about a year before. We had kept in touch after her conversion and would talk on the phone from time to time. About a month earlier I had asked her to pray for me because I couldn't decide if God wanted me to be a priest or to get married. She had been praying for me and now she was calling to tell me something important. She asked me to meet her at a restaurant because she wanted to talk to me in person.

I went to meet her with some apprehension because I didn't know what she was going to tell me. What she told me was pretty amazing. She told me that she often went to Holy Mass during her lunch hour because there was a Catholic Church right across the street from her downtown office that had a daily noon Mass. Normally, she went alone, but a few days before our meeting one of the other women in the office said that she would like to go along with Jane to Mass. The lady was not a Catholic, but she thought it would be a good place to pray. When Mass was over they left the church and began to walk back to their office when the lady asked Jane, "Do you have a friend who can't decide whether he should become a priest or get married?"

Jane almost fainted with surprise. She answered that she did have such a friend and that she had been praying for him during Mass.

The lady told Jane that while she was praying in Church the Lord had spoken to her and said, "Tell Jane to tell her friend who can't decide between priesthood and marriage, that it's okay for him to get married. I have plenty of work for him to do."

Wow! You talk about a sign from God. A complete stranger gets a direct answer from God for your question. That's even better than God speaking directly to me because I might have had some doubts that maybe I was just imagining an answer from God. But this answer came from a person who knew absolutely nothing about me or my dilemma so I could really put faith in it. I thanked Jane for her prayers and for passing on the message. Joyously, I drove back to Sidney to share this good news with Ann.

God gave us another sign the next day. As I was leaving the prayer meeting, a woman who was also walking out to the parking lot, mentioned to me that she had a dream the night before and that in her dream I had gotten married. When I asked her who I had married in her dream, she replied, "Ann Fisher." She didn't realize at all how prophetic her dream would prove to be.

I was very grateful that God had given me such clear and dramatic signs on this important matter of my vocation because I really needed it. I don't think I would have been able to proceed without it. It's been my experience that God always gives us what we need, though not always what we want.

Now that we had God's approval, Ann and I made plans for our wedding. We were married at Holy Angels Church on November 24, 1978, and that began a whole new life for both of us.

On our honeymoon (which we spent at my apartment because I had pneumonia on our wedding day and was too sick to travel) we sat on the couch one evening and asked God to give us a Scripture passage that would be the theme of our married life. With my eyes closed I opened the Bible at random and placed my finger on the page (some people call this practice "Bible Roulette"). The passage it landed on was the one where Jesus compared the Kingdom of God to a mustard seed, which starts out very small but grows into a large shrub and the birds of the air make their nests in its branches. We had no idea how that verse would play itself out in our future, but we were ready to begin.

Married Life

When we were first married, Ann and I knew we wanted children but didn't know how many so we prayed and asked God for an answer. The next day I asked Ann if God had given her an answer, and she said that God had told her seven children. I had received the exact same number in prayer also. This was kind of a shock to me because I had never thought of having a large family, and in fact I didn't even like kids that much. But God had told us what He wanted so we started down the road with the goal of having seven children.

Soon we were blessed with our first child who was due to arrive on our first wedding anniversary. As we made plans for the baby's arrival, a house came for sale on the market. It was an old fixer-upper that was in the same neighborhood where we were living at that time. I asked my Dad to come and inspect the house with us one evening. My Dad had been an excellent carpenter so

I wanted his opinion about the house. After the realtor had finished showing us the house, my Dad told me not to buy it. I was surprised because I thought it was a pretty good deal from what I had seen. Dad proceeded to point out major flaws in the foundation of the house that could cause big problems in the future. Immediately, I was convinced by his opinion and gave no further thought to buying that house because when it came to construction I trusted my Dad's opinion more than my own.

My Friend, do you trust your heavenly Father more than yourself? You should, you know. We often want to run our own lives and attempt to be in control of everything. If we would only turn to God, our heavenly Father, and ask Him what He thinks of our plans and then follow His advice, our lives would be so much better. God knows everything about us and loves us perfectly. There is really no reason not to trust Him completely in every aspect of our lives yet so few people really live that way. The ones who do find great joy and security knowing that whatever God wants will be in their best interest. It wasn't hard for me to follow my Dad's advice concerning that house because I knew that Dad's advice was in my best interest. Similarly, it's not hard to follow God's will when you trust Him with all your heart. So my Friend, stop trying to run your own life. Submit your plans to God and seek His advice. Then you will be able to proceed in complete confidence knowing that you are doing God's will and not just your own.

Soon another old fixer-upper came on the market, and with Dad's approval I bought it. With three months until Ann's due date, I began to fix up a nursery room for the baby.

Everything went well with Ann's pregnancy and our first child, Maria, was born a week before our first anniversary. The birth of a baby is such a miracle, and it really hits you when that little baby is your own. Instantly, I began to love kids!

Covenant House

At that time there were some covenant communities forming within the Catholic Charismatic Renewal in various cities around the nation. We read about these in some books and magazines and even visited one in Ann Arbor, Michigan.

We learned about some interesting things happening in these covenant communities that we thought we would like to imitate in our own home. Rose was a young single woman in our prayer group who shared our vision, and with her we began our own covenant household. It was our attempt to try to combine some of the good facets of life in a religious order with ordinary family life.

We shared expenses and ate supper together each day. We had evening prayers in common and did a lot of household chores together. Rose was a help to us, and we were able to free up some of her time so that she could serve the larger community. Rose lived with us for two years, and I think it worked out well for all of us. During the second year a young man from the prayer group also moved into our big old house. He had been struggling with some issues in life and was not living in a healthy environment. We saw his joining us as a way that we could minister to his needs by just being a loving family environment for him. He spent a year with us. Overall it helped him greatly, but there were definitely some challenging moments of pain to overcome. By this time our second child, Ruth, had arrived. The mustard seed that began with Ann and I had certainly grown a lot.

Unwed Mothers

One Saturday morning I stayed in church after Mass to spend some time praying and reading. As I was reading a Catholic newspaper suddenly the Lord spoke to my mind and said, "I want you to take unwed mothers into your home."

This message really jolted me because it just came out of the blue. I hadn't given any thought to doing such a thing and wasn't even asking God a question. But as I thought about it, it seemed like a really good thing to do. Ann and I had become very pro-life after our conversions and wanted to do whatever we could to stop babies from being murdered by abortion.

I went home and discussed with Ann and Rose the possibility of taking in unwed mothers who needed a place to live. We thought it would be a very charitable thing to do, and we still had some empty rooms in our house. To make sure I wasn't being foolish, I ran the idea past Fr. Jim and explained its origin. He also thought it was a good idea so we decided to give it a try. I contacted the local Catholic Social Services agency and told them that we would be willing to take an unwed mother into our home. Within a month they sent us our first girl, Robin. She stayed with us for about six months and delivered a beautiful baby girl, which she allowed to be adopted by a loving family. Everything went well with Robin, and we eventually hosted eight unwed mothers in six years. During that same period of time Ann was having four babies of our own. Our house was full of mothers and babies and was often quite a circus. Looking back I don't know how we managed it all. I'm sure it was God's grace that carried us through.

One day the neighbor lady asked me, "Who in the hell are all those people at your house everyday?" I explained that some were members of our covenant household and that others were unwed mothers and some were their friends from the streets. I remember one summer when Ann was cooking for nine or ten people every day for supper. She did an incredible amount of work. The neighbors thought we were crazy, but we saw ourselves as just trying to be pro-life and sharing what we had.

Earthquake!

Paula was an unwed mother who stayed with us during her pregnancy, who had a friend from the streets named Terri who often stopped in to visit. Terri was also pregnant so we invited her to move in with us, but she refused. She was living here and there and her life was chaotic. We wanted her to come to supper each day so that she would get at least one nutritious meal a day. She showed up most days.

One Sunday morning Paula told us that Terri had decided to abort her baby. She didn't have a reason other than she just didn't want to be pregnant anymore. We asked Paula when Terri was planning to do this. She told us that Terri was going to Cincinnati on a bus that evening and would get the abortion on Monday morning.

Of course we wanted to stop her from doing this terrible deed, but we had to find her in order to talk to her. Paula told us where Terri sometimes spent the night, and Ann and I drove there to look for her. The house was a dump and when someone let us in we found the worst living conditions imaginable. There were more than thirty cats roaming around the house, resulting in cat feces everywhere. The stench was overpowering. In fact, Ann was holding our little two-year old daughter Maria and within thirty seconds the little child began to gag and vomit. Later we found out that the health department had condemned the house. No one there knew where Terri was so we continued searching for her by driving around the downtown area.

Our search proved futile so we went back home about noon. To our surprise, Paula showed up with Terri an hour later. We sat in the living room and talked with Terri and did our best to help her choose life for her baby. I went to the kitchen and phoned a prayer group family and asked them to pray immediately for this situation and to spread the word.

Ann and Paula continued to try to reason with Terri and to use every means possible to persuade her not to have an abortion, but Terri refused to change her mind. I was listening and praying fervently that somehow we would be able to get through to her because a baby's life hung in the balance. Then it happened. The house started to shake!

I yelled, "It's an earthquake!" and told everyone to run out of the house into the yard. The tremor lasted about thirty seconds and then stopped. That was the only time in my life that I've ever felt an earthquake of any size. The newspaper reported it the next day and stated that it was just a tremor.

After a few minutes we thought it was safe and went back into the house. Once again we tried to talk Terri out of the abortion. I told her that God had shaken the earth in an attempt to get her attention and make her realize the importance of what she was planning to do. I told her that the earthquake was not just a coincidence but a sign from God to her that He was displeased with her intention to abort and was trying to stop her.

It seemed like our message was starting to get through to Terri. When we finished our conversation Paula and Terri went for a walk. Many hours passed and they still hadn't returned. Finally, later that evening we received a call from Paula who was calling from a pay phone in Cincinnati. She told us that Terri had gone straight from our house to the bus station and bought herself a ticket to Cincinnati, where she planned to get an abortion the next morning. Our attempts at persuading her to choose life had failed.

Paula told us that she had had enough money with her to buy a bus ticket and that she was not going to give up the fight, but stay with Terri and keep trying to stop her. We were very happy that Paula was still with Terri and doing her best. On our end, we had everyone praying for them.

Terri's appointment for the abortion was early on Monday morning. Paula kept talking to Terri as they walked down the sidewalk to the abortion center, but Terri wouldn't change her mind. As they neared the center, Paula got the idea to invite Terri to breakfast. She knew that Terri loved to eat, and Paula said that she would buy breakfast for her. In this way, she hoped to stall Terri and buy more time to talk her out of the abortion.

Terri loved to eat and couldn't refuse a free meal so off they went for breakfast. Paula stalled her at breakfast for as long as she could, but eventually Terri headed back to the abortion center. Paula, who was at her wits end, walked beside her as they came to the door of the center.

At the door Terri hesitated and then stopped. She didn't open the door. She turned to Paula and began to share her thoughts and feelings, her fears and worries. Paula was there for her and was able to help her choose life. They decided to get on a bus and come back home. The child's life was spared.

When they showed up at our house and told us what had happened, we all embraced and praised the Lord. God's grace had melted Terri's heart, and she just couldn't go through with it.

One of the important lessons to be learned from this story is the power of friendship. We have learned that the most important need of a woman facing a crisis pregnancy is friendship. The power of another person is incredibly important in facing difficulties in life. By ourselves we can easily fall prey to fears, whether real or imagined, and then panic and make all kinds of destructive decisions. It's an altogether different dynamic at work when we have a friend by our side. Their friendship helps us to see clearly and makes us much braver in facing difficulties and dangers.

Pro-Lifers everywhere need to know that the most powerful tool they have to stop abortion on a one-to-one level is their friendship. If you come across someone who is contemplating aborting her child, you need to immediately assure that woman that you will be her friend and that you will walk with her and help her to bring this new life into the world. She needs to know that she will be able to depend on you for whatever needs may arise and that you will not abandon her for any reason. That kind of friendship and commitment has the power to change mothers' lives and to save babies from abortion. Don't be afraid to be a friend to that person who needs you because Jesus will be walking with both of you.

Finally, a footnote to this story. On the afternoon of the earthquake/tremor, I had spoken very confidently to Terri, telling her that God had shaken the earth to send her a message. That evening before I went to bed, I spent some time in prayer. I asked God if I had spoken correctly and if it really was Him who had sent the tremor. I opened my Bible at random and the first verse on the page was: *"As they prayed, the place where they were gathered shook."*

Tough Love

The most memorable of all the girls who came to live with us was Shannon. She was twenty-two years old and originally from Dayton, Ohio, which was about forty miles away. She had a troubled youth and her parents had given up on her. She had spent some time in the Navy but had been kicked out because she wouldn't get out of bed in the morning. She was lazy and irresponsible to an extreme. She had lived in Philadelphia and San Diego and lots of places in-between. Now she was homeless and pregnant so we welcomed her into our home. Shannon had one abortion previously. It had been a terrible experience that she never wanted to repeat. This time she planned to give birth to her baby and then allow a family to adopt the child. It was a good plan, and we tried to help her achieve it.

Living with Shannon was difficult because of her irresponsible nature. She just about drove Ann crazy. One memorable evening Ann came marching into Holy Angels School where I was teaching a New Life in the Spirit class. She had a baby on her hip and a toddler by her side, and she blasted me with the news that Shannon had overflowed the bathtub and that there was water all over the floor of the bathroom and the kitchen. She also informed me that I had better go home immediately and "do something about that girl" or else she was going to take the kids and move to the Holiday Inn. Ann was really angry, and I immediately went home to try to resolve the crisis. Living with Shannon seemed to be an endless series of crises, but slowly we made progress in helping her to behave in a more mature fashion.

She had several wounds from her past that needed healing, and I spent many evenings talking with her for hours. The ultimate answer for many of her issues was a relationship with Jesus as her Lord and Savior. Day after day I taught and explained to her the way of the Lord and a desire for Jesus began to grow within her heart. She very much admired and desired the kind of family life that we had, full of love and acceptance and joy. Her family life had been one of war and division. She didn't know that life could be so different. I taught her that Jesus was the difference maker because Ann and I had both given our hearts and lives to Christ. Personal peace of heart makes peaceful relationships with others possible.

After a few months, Shannon wanted that peace of heart that only Jesus can give. One evening we prayed with her as she committed her life to Jesus and asked to be filled with the Holy Spirit. That was a big turning point for her. She had been baptized into the Catholic Church as an infant but had not practiced the faith since early childhood. I told her to make a good, general confession of her life so that she could start over spiritually in the state of grace, and she did. Then she began to go to Mass each Sunday with us and joined us in our daily prayers at home. She was making good spiritual progress.

This type of spiritual progress happened with most of the girls who lived with us, but not all. Usually the experience of living in a loving, Catholic family that was overtly religious had a profound effect upon them. They wanted the joy and peace that they saw in our lives, and we were able to lead them to Jesus, who is the source of all love, joy, and peace.

Our years of experience of serving unwed mothers in our home has convinced us that many wounded people will only find the healing they need by moving into a whole new environment. If a child or an adult is living in a terrible environment that has caused mental or emotional instability, then that person needs much more than counseling can provide. Even though the counseling may be very good, they are still living in an unsuitable environment that caused the problem in the first place. They need a new, loving, healthy environment where they can learn to live in a new way. When the physical environment and the spiritual environment are both working properly, it is amazing how persons can grow and thrive and become the beautiful persons that God had intended when He created them.

Dear Friend, there is a great need in our world for this type of service to others. Could you provide a whole new environment for someone? Is your home full of the love of the Lord, a love that could heal all the wounds that someone has suffered? If you can, consider taking someone into your home. St. James taught, *"True religion is taking care of orphans and widows in their need."* There are many kinds of orphans and widows today if we have the eyes to see them. Some of them are not far from you. Look for them and love them, for in loving them you are loving Jesus Himself. *"I was a stranger and you welcomed me."*

Eventually Shannon gave birth to a beautiful baby boy. All of the legal arrangements for the baby's adoption had been completed, and after a few days the adoption was finalized. It is not easy for a mother to allow her baby to be adopted by another couple, but it is often the most loving choice that can be made for the child. This was the difficult but loving choice that the more mature girls who had lived with us made. The more immature ones kept their babies to raise on their own and this usually did not turn out very well.

Most of our girls had moved out of our home after a few weeks of recuperation, but Shannon wanted to stay with us. She had become somewhat attached to us and thought she could grow spiritually by living with us. We agreed that she could stay, but there would have to be some new conditions.

All of our pregnant girls stayed with us completely free of charge, and we never took any money from the government. While they were with us they were considered part of the family. But if Shannon was going to stay with us, she would have to work. St. Paul taught, *"Those who will not work should not eat."* Allowing a healthy adult to just lie around the house would be promoting laziness and immaturity.

Shannon didn't know where to get a job so I asked a friend who was in charge of a nearby nursing home if she could work as an aide there. She could walk to work, which was good because she didn't have a car, and the job was a typical entry-level job. Everything went well for awhile.

But Shannon had a problem getting out of bed in the morning. Her problem was that she liked to sleep too much! This is what had gotten her kicked out of the Navy, and now it was threatening her job. Several times she was late for work, and the boss was not happy. Eventually, she was told that if she missed work again she would be fired. Ann and I talked repeatedly with Shannon about this issue and did our best to get her out of bed and off to work. I remember one morning taking her by the arm and actually pulling her out of bed until she fell onto the floor because she simply wouldn't get up.

As you could probably guess, Shannon eventually got fired from her job for not showing up for work. She was an adult, and we couldn't treat her as a kid and always be forcing her out the door and off to work. We had put reasonable expectations upon her, but she had failed to meet them. Something was going to have to change if she was going to continue living with us.

But nothing did change. I told her to get another job and keep it or else she would have to move out. She made very little effort to find a job so I did what I felt I had to do. On the cold morning of the second of January, I put her few clothes in a suitcase and placed it on the sidewalk in front of our house. Then I escorted her to the front sidewalk where we said goodbye. It was too bad that it had to end that way but her actions had forced me to throw her out. It was the loving thing to do. Sometimes love must be tough.

She didn't know what to do so I told her that she needed to hitch a ride to her parents' home in Dayton, and when she got there she should beg for their forgiveness for all the problems that she had caused during her teenage years. I really thought that it was important for her to mend the relationship with her parents if she wanted to grow spiritually. With that advice I walked back into the house and closed the door.

Three weeks later there was a knock on our front door. There stood Shannon. She said that she wanted to thank us for loving her enough to throw her out. What we had done had made her face up to her past mistakes and face her parents. She had done exactly what I had told her to do. She hitched a ride to her parents' house and knocked on the front door. Her Dad opened the door, saw his daughter that he hadn't seen for four years, and then closed the door in her face without saying a word. Shannon knocked again. This time her Mother opened the door and let her in. Straightaway she apologized for all that she had done wrong. She truly humbled herself before them and tried to begin the reconciliation process.

Her parents allowed her to stay, and they began to patch up what had been an extremely rocky relationship. Shannon told us that she had gotten a job and had been on time every day and was doing well at work. She even had some plans for her future and had come back to say thanks.

Needless to say we were overjoyed to hear that she was walking in the right direction. We encouraged her to keep up the good work and to stay in touch. She told us that it was hard and that her parents were still pretty cold and skeptical towards her, but that she was going to keep trying to do her best.

She did phone us from time to time and slowly her life improved. She met a good Christian man, and after dating him for about a year, they decided to get married. As they made wedding plans, Shannon's parents informed her that they would have nothing to do with her wedding and wouldn't even attend it. This lack of forgiveness on their part was heartbreaking to her, but she could console herself with the thought that she had tried to reconcile. She had repented, but they hadn't forgiven her. You can't force someone to love you or to forgive you; it must come from their heart.

With her parents unwilling to co-operate, Shannon turned to us. She asked Ann to be her matron of honor and asked me to do the duties of the father of the bride and to walk her down the aisle. We quickly agreed and even volunteered our two little daughters to be flower girls. Her wedding day turned out to be a wonderful occasion and many tears of joy were shed, as should be the case when families love one another.

Our years of hosting unwed mothers eventually came to an end when we moved to my hometown of Russia. All the rooms of our new house were filled with our own seven children. Looking back on those years, it's easy to see how the mustard seed passage that God had given us when we were first married was being fulfilled. Eight different birds had come and made their nests in our branches. But they weren't the only ones to find love and shelter in our home.

Addicted

My brother Joe was addicted to Valium for over twenty years. It had started with a doctor's prescription but became a severe addiction involving lots of unlawful activities. When he over-dosed and was taken to the emergency room of the hospital, we searched his car and found thousands of Valium pills. After forty days of detoxification at the hospital, he was released and needed somewhere to go. He couldn't go home because my elderly Dad was unable to care for him. So we took him into our home.

His physical condition was a wreck. His eyes wouldn't focus properly and for the next month he couldn't read the headlines in the local newspaper. His balance was so shaky that he could barely walk. He went up and down the stairs in our home sitting down and scooting on his butt like a child. I had to put food on his plate because his hands shook so badly that if he tried to serve himself, the food would spill all over the table. The drugs had certainly taken a terrible toll upon his body.

His mental condition wasn't much better. He had always suffered from some mental illness, but the drug abuse had certainly aggravated it. He had delusions of grandeur that handicapped him from dealing with reality.

I zeroed in on his spiritual condition. I wanted to use this opportunity to bring him to the Lord who was the only one who could deal with the mess that he had made of his life. I told him all about my own conversion and how the Lord had freed me from alcohol. Daily we encouraged him to turn to Jesus in all of his problems.

Slowly his physical health began to improve, and we had many serious spiritual discussions. I answered all of his questions and concerns to the best of my ability. He could see that Jesus was the answer to all that he hoped and longed for in life. At my urging he made a general confession of his life of sin and turned his heart to Jesus. We prayed over him to be filled with the Holy Spirit, and he began a new life in Christ. He never took drugs again. In fact, a few years later he told me that he wouldn't take drugs even if someone tried to pay him to do so. Jesus said, *"If the Son sets you free, you are free indeed."* That was the case with Joe and the Valium that he had been addicted to for so long.

Although he was free from drugs, he still struggled with some other aspects of his life, especially due to his life-long mental illness. But through it all he had learned how to praise the Lord and was faithful to the practices of the Catholic Church. In 2004, he died suddenly of a heart attack. May he rest in peace.

Les Miserables

There was yet another bird who nested in our branches during our nine years of living in Sidney. His name was John.

A small alley separated our home from a big old house on the other side. John lived upstairs with Tom, his widowed Dad, and his older brother and sister. Tom's brother Ron, his wife, and daughter lived in the lower portion of the house. They were transplants from the hills of Kentucky who had come north to find factory work.

Ron's family were fundamentalist Christians and very active in their church. Tom's family was completely different. They had no religion at all and were completely dysfunctional. I felt sympathy for them.

Tom worked long hours at a factory and spent the rest of his time drinking. His alcoholism had completely destroyed his ability to interact with others in any meaningful way. He would sit on the step of his house for hours and stare into space. When I would say hi or greet him, he sometimes replied with a grunt but usually didn't even do that.

The oldest boy was in jail by the time he was seventeen and the daughter was pregnant by sixteen. It was sad to watch this self-destruction next door.

John was about eleven when we moved in next door. He was angry, *very angry*. You could see it in his eyes and in how he walked and talked. There was evil in that young boy, and it was growing. And who could blame him for his anger. His situation would have made anyone angry.

His Dad did not give him a key to the house, so when he came home he had to wait for someone to let him in. Often there was no one home so he waited a long time. Other times his knocking was ignored and he might wait for an hour for someone to come down the stairs and let him in. By the way, he didn't knock the way you or I would. In order to get someone's attention he would turn his back to the steel door and slam the sole of his foot against it repeatedly. It was very loud but it didn't do him much good. The response was always very slow.

One day he stood in the rain waiting for someone to unlock the door. I saw him and invited him to come across the alley to sit on our porch while he waited. We talked and got to know each other a little.

A strong relationship would develop from that small beginning. Our home, our love, and Ann's cooking became a magnet that drew John into our lives. Before long it seemed like he was always at our house, and we were glad to have him around because we could see the slow transformation going on in his life. The evil and anger in his eyes were slowly being replaced by happiness.

As with any adolescent there were some ups and downs. Once he stole twenty dollars out of the money jar in our kitchen. We had to work our way through that episode and teach him to be honest. We taught him to be respectful and to be helpful. He was really a good kid who just needed the right loving environment, and I thank God that we were able to provide it for him.

No one in his family had ever graduated from high school. We encouraged him to do well in school and take an interest in his schoolwork. He was doing okay in school and was hoping to graduate, but he dropped out when he was sixteen and had gotten his driver's license. He couldn't overcome the lure of making money at a job. He found a job at a local lumber company and soon was driving a delivery truck for them.

Eventually we moved from Sidney and lost track of John. The last we heard of him, he was happily married, the father of a child, and was driving a truck for his living. We are so happy that he was able to live a normal life. I'm convinced that without our intervention in his life he would have spent much of his life in prison or worse. There are some things in life that you feel really good about. You're really glad that God gave you the chance to be a part of it. Well, we're really glad and thank God for letting us be a part of John's life and helping to bring a smile to his face that was so full of pain. More than any other time in my life I felt like the Bishop in Les Miserables who said to Jean Valjean, "My brother, you belong no longer to evil, but to good. It is your soul that I am buying for you. I withdraw it from dark thoughts and from the spirit of evil and I give it to God!" And the great thing about what we were able to do for John was that all we did was be ourselves and include him in our family life. Anybody could have done the same thing; it just takes the willingness to include someone outside your comfort zone into your life.

Painting for Souls

John and Deb had been good friends and classmates of Ann in high school. As we were beginning our married life in Sidney, they were raising their young children in a home only a few blocks away. They invited us over one Saturday evening to socialize and catch up on their old friendship. We discussed mostly secular topics, but we did talk a little about spiritual things. They seemed to be open to what we were saying about the Lord. As we drove home I mentioned to Ann that I saw a lot of potential in them.

A few months later we were driving past their home and saw John on a ladder scraping off some old paint from his house. It looked like he was preparing to paint his large old house which was going to be a big job. Ann told me that this was my chance to try to convert John. She said that I should volunteer to help John paint his house. During the hours we spent painting, I would be able to talk to John about the new life in the Spirit. I didn't really want to spend my evenings painting someone else's house, but I knew she had a good idea. I would have to do some work, but it would be a perfect opportunity for evangelism.

The next day I showed up with my scraper and paint brush and told John that I would help him. He was pretty surprised at first but was more than glad to have my help. So for the next two weeks we spent each evening painting and talking about the Lord.

He was very interested to hear all about my conversion and how the Holy Spirit had been poured into my life. He had been a life-long Catholic but wasn't on fire with the Holy Spirit. As we talked he began to develop a desire for a deeper, more personal relationship with Jesus. I explained the new life in the Spirit as best as I could and answered his concerns.

By the time we finished painting the house, John was ready to surrender his life to Christ. We sat at the picnic table in his back yard as we prayed together. He committed his entire life into God's hands, and we prayed for the outpouring of the Holy Spirit. Right there in his back yard he experienced his own Pentecost as his soul was flooded with the joy, peace, and the power of the Holy Spirit. He had been set on fire and has been burning ever since! He shared his new relationship with Christ with his wife Deb, and soon thereafter she followed his lead and also experienced the Baptism in the Holy Spirit.

Although they moved to Oregon not long after that, we have always remained good friends with a spiritual bond between us all. They have grown strong in the Spirit and have been a source of spiritual strength and evangelism to many people over the past thirty years.

My Friend, are you willing to do some work in order to spread the faith? Yes, it often takes time and effort to do the will of God, and if we're lazy we won't do it. Almost all of us could serve God more in some way, but our laziness prevents us. How much time have you wasted on useless activities? Make a resolution today that you will improve your use of time and that you will work more in the service of God; you'll be glad you did. I'll be forever thankful that I spent a couple of weeks painting a house because I was rewarded with the beautiful friendship of a new brother and sister in Christ. Our time on this earth is limited for all of us. Each day is a gift and an opportunity. Jesus said, *"Let us work while it is day for the night cometh when no man can work."* Don't waste the time you've been given but use it wisely for God. The rewards are eternal.

You've Got to be Kidding!

In the spring of 1980 I began to have an interior sense that God wanted me to get a new job. I had been working with the mentally retarded and developmentally disabled at S&H products for about three years, and I liked my job and loved the people there. I knew that what I was doing was a really good way to serve the Lord, but I had a persistent interior sense that God had something else for me to do.

Everyday I would ask God what he wanted me to do, but there was no answer. Occasionally, I perused the classified ads in the newspaper looking for a different job. Nothing seemed to fit. I really had no clue what job God had in mind for me so I just kept on asking for an answer in prayer. This situation went on for about a year.

On the morning of May 18, 1981, I was sitting in a chair in my bedroom saying my usual morning prayers. Like hundreds of times before, I asked God what he wanted me to do. This time there was an immediate answer. God spoke to me in a manner that was as clear as if a voice was coming through an intercom speaker in the ceiling. It was that clear and unmistakable.

God said to me, "I want you to go to Lehman and teach religion."

Immediately, I responded aloud, "You've got to be kidding," but there was no response. Immediately, my mind started to analyze what God had told me, and my reaction was very negative.

Lehman was a local Catholic High School in Sidney. I didn't know much about the school, but I did know that I didn't want to be a teacher in any school. My only experience being a teacher had been extremely negative and painful. I had quit the job after only two weeks and never wanted to go through that again. So when God told me to be a teacher at Lehman, I thought it was about the worst possible job that He could have told me to do. But I had accepted Jesus as my Lord, which means that

He had complete rule over my life, and if He was commanding me to be a teacher then I would have to obey Him no matter how much I hated the thought of it.

As I sat rather stunned in my bedroom, I told the Lord that I would obey His command, but I needed to know for sure that this was His will because it certainly was not mine. I asked God to confirm His message by giving me some sort of sign. Only then would I act upon the message.

A couple of days later I received a phone call from my friend John who was living in Portland, Oregon. He had moved there a few years before to take a job as an investment banker, and he and his family were doing fine. His call surprised me because we hadn't spoken together for a couple of years.

He told me that something quite remarkable had happened and that he wanted my opinion. He said that God had spoken to him in prayer and had told him to go to Lehman and teach business. He was shocked by this message and wanted my discernment about it.

I told John that God had just spoken to me and told me to go to Lehman and teach religion! We were both astounded by what had happened and concluded that it was God's will for us to go to Lehman and teach. We agreed that we would each call Fr. Denis, who was the principal at Lehman, and apply for teaching positions.

I called Fr. Denis and told him how God had spoken to me in prayer and called me to teach religion at Lehman. Father knew me from daily Mass and we were on friendly terms with each other. He told me that he appreciated my interest in the school, but that he had already hired the religion teachers for the next year and so there was no opening at that time. When John called Fr. Denis, he received the same reply. There wasn't an opening for a business teacher either.

John and I had done our part; now we had to let it in God's hands. If God wanted us there He would have to make it happen because we couldn't do any more about it.

My wife's ten-year class reunion was approaching on July 25th. In her prayers she had asked God to let us know by that day if I was going to be a teacher at Lehman or not, so that she would be able to tell her classmates what her husband's occupation was when they would ask at the reunion.

On July 20th I received a phone call from Fr. Denis while I was working at S&H Products. He said, "Henry, you'll never guess what happened. One of my religion teachers just quit. Would you be interested in the job?"

I told him that I'd drive right over and talk with him. I'll bet that not too many teachers ever showed up for their job interview wearing jeans and a tee shirt like I did that day. I was very relaxed as I answered the questions posed to me by the three administrators. I knew that they were going to hire me because God had told me back in May. The interview ended, and Fr. Denis said that he would call me later with his decision. A few days later I signed my teaching contract with Lehman. It was July 24th, just one day before the deadline that my wife had asked God to meet.

You might be wondering if John got a job at Lehman also. No, he didn't. There was never an opening. We talked about it later and came to the conclusion that God was using the message to John as a sign for me. God never really wanted John to teach at Lehman, but He gave him that message as a way of confirming what He had spoken to me.

John's part in this whole affair teaches us a great spiritual lesson, namely, that we must always follow God's inspiration, even if it seems rather foolish because we are all just a singular piece of a much larger puzzle. When John received his message in prayer, it must have seemed quite ridiculous to him to think that God wanted him to move his family from Oregon to Ohio and for him to change careers with a seventy-five percent loss of salary in order to teach in a Catholic high school. As ridiculous as it seemed, he still acted upon this inspiration and called me for advice because he thought it was from God and he was committed to doing God's will. He had no idea at the time that he was playing a part in a much bigger picture that only God could see. By following the inspiration he had received, he was able to cooperate with God's larger plan about which he had no knowledge.

This is how all of our lives are used by God. Each moment in each day of our lives is a piece of the jigsaw puzzle. Take a single piece of a complex jigsaw puzzle and examine it closely. Can you determine what the whole picture is from that single piece? Of course not! And the individual events of our lives are like those individual pieces of the puzzle. Most of the time we really don't know the eternal value and meaning of what we do or don't do in this life. At best, we occasionally catch a partial glimpse of the bigger picture.

We need to follow the call and inspiration of God at every moment in our lives with the complete trust that God, who knows the end and the beginning at the same time, is guiding us to fulfill His larger plan for the salvation of the whole world. And do not think that the call of God is normally something dramatic or spectacular, for that is not the case. Most of the time, God's call and will for our lives simply demands that we do the daily duties of our state in life with all of the holiness and faithfulness that we can muster. I can't emphasize this truth enough. Some people are always chasing after some sort of spiritual excitement or miraculous event. That kind of spiritual ambulance chasing should not be the focus of our life. We should be fulfilling God's plan for our lives in our daily routine of prayer and work.

There can be moments of spectacular spiritual activity in our lives, but it is not for us to try to make those happen. When God wants the miraculous to occur He will send it into our lives; our part is to be open to whatever He wants to send to us. In this book I have recounted for you many spectacular workings of God the Holy Spirit in my life and in people close to me. I don't want you to get the impression that my life has been a continuous series of spectacular spiritual interventions of God's power. The vast majority of my life has been very routine and average. But I have learned that God is just as active in my life in my daily routine of prayer and work as He is when I'm involved in a healing, or an exorcism, or in the conversion of someone.

You should not be surprised to find God in your daily routine. When God came to earth in the person of Jesus, He spent thirty of His thirty-three years living an average life with His family and doing His daily work. During all of those years at home, He was just as much God as He was during His public ministry. He was just as much God when He was sawing a board or carrying a bucket of water at home, as when He was curing a leper or changing water into wine or preaching the Kingdom of God. At all times He was the same Jesus, the same God.

So too in our lives. We fulfill God's plan for us at every moment of each day. We can't even begin to see the big picture of which we are each a part. We leave that to God, trusting that as we respond to the grace and inspiration of the Holy Spirit at each moment, He is using us to create something very beautiful that we will see and understand in heaven. As St. Paul taught, *"Eye has not seen, ear has not heard, nor has it entered into the mind of man, what God has prepared for those who love Him."*

Survival

The first year of teaching is usually a pretty tough experience for most teachers, and my first year at Lehman certainly fit that description. In fact, it was downright brutal.

There was a group of senior boys who thought it was fun to pick out a teacher and then harass that person until he quit his job. They would then pick another teacher and start the process over again. The year before I came to Lehman, one religion teacher quit by Thanksgiving and another one quit at the end of the school year. Several years later one of the boys in that group told me that they had picked me as their target on the first day of school and had tried their best to drive me out of school.

I was harassed in many ways both day and night. They would call my home at 3:00 A.M. and scream obscenities at me on the phone. They vandalized my car and my house. They would yell insults from crowded hallways, and I even received written death threats. This type of harassment went on everyday.

Besides the harassment, I had all the normal struggles of making new preparations for several different classes each day and preparing tests and quizzes for the first time. Also, when someone first starts to teach, they make a lot of errors in how they present the material and how they discipline the students. The more mistakes you make, the more difficult that first year becomes.

It didn't take long until I definitely wanted to quit, and I would have quit if I hadn't been there for a reason. First, the Lord had specifically commanded me to teach at Lehman High School so I knew it was His will that I stay there, and since He is my Lord and Savior, I must do His will with all my heart and strength, even if it entails suffering and death. Secondly, the love and support of my wife, Ann, pulled me through. Without her I am certain that I wouldn't have finished the year. I probably would have had a nervous breakdown and just collapsed. It's amazing to me how much stronger I've become in every way because of our marriage. When two people are joined together their strength more than doubles; it grows exponentially. Each person finds that they can achieve far more than they have ever thought possible because someone else joins them in the effort. I would imagine that's why Jesus always sent out his disciples in pairs. He knew that the power of two people working together far exceeds what they could do individually. Jesus even made a comment on the power of two people praying together, saying that He would be present with them.

In my heart I know that it was my relationship with Ann that enabled me to survive that first year at Lehman. The second year and every year since has been much better. Now I'm in my twenty-seventh year of teaching religion at Lehman High School. I love my job, and I love my students. They treat me with love and respect, making it is such a joy to pass on the Catholic Faith to them each day.

As I've said before, God knows everything. He knew me better than I knew myself. He knew that He had given me a gift to teach and that I would enjoy it. I thought that I never wanted to try teaching again because of my first awful experience with it, but God knew better than me. When He told me to go to Lehman I thought it was going to be the worst job in the world, but it has turned out to be the perfect job for me.

My Friend, God knows you better than you know yourself. He knows what will bring you the greatest joy in this life and what will lead you to eternal life. If you follow His calling, it will be Heaven all the way to Heaven because you'll be walking with Jesus all the time.

How can you know God's calling for your life? Pray, pray, pray! Constantly ask God to lead you in the path that He desires. Keep your heart open to doing His will at all times. Practice the basics of the Catholic Faith and keep yourself in the state of grace. Try to serve God and others by doing good deeds. As you go about living your life in this way you can be sure that God will guide you into your vocation. He will speak to you through the circumstances of life that arise and through doors of opportunity that open and close. Sometimes He will guide you with pain and suffering. What's most important is that your heart always remains open and willing to accept whatever God wants for you. If you trust in Jesus' love for you, your heart will always be open to His will. It's a good practice to pray these words in your heart several times a day, "Jesus, I trust in You!"

Part VI
Defending Life

Pro-life Dream

God spoke to me in a dream during the night of February 18, 1982. In the dream, my wife and I and some others were standing at the edge of a huge cornfield and were watching the corn being harvested. There was a large eight-row combine harvesting the abundant crop. The wagons were overflowing with corn, and there was an atmosphere of joy.

Then as the combine turned around to pick another eight rows, I saw some children playing by the corn. One boy was standing right in the row in front of the combine. We yelled for him to jump out of the way, but the noise was too great and he didn't hear us. The driver didn't see him and ran over the boy with the combine. The driver didn't know this had happened and just kept on driving. I ran to the child who was lying face down in the field. I turned him over to see if he was alive or dead, and as his body rolled over, his head fell back and blood began to pour from his throat. I quickly tried to find the artery and to put pressure on it to stop the bleeding. I knew he would be dead in just a few seconds if I didn't stop the bleeding.

As I frantically tried to find the artery to put pressure on it, I prayed to God to please help me quickly. Immediately, I found the artery and stopped the bleeding. I shouted for someone to get the rescue squad as I stayed with the boy. As I knelt there alone over the boy, I could see that his neck wound was the only wound on his body. It amazed me that this was his only wound after being run over by the huge combine.

As I looked at him, he was still breathing, but he looked in very bad condition. Even if help came, I didn't think he had much chance to live. I continued to kneel there and apply pressure to stop the bleeding and hoped that help would come and save him.

As I waited for help, I wondered if the boy had ever been baptized a Christian. Since I had no water to baptize with, I made the Sign of the Cross on his forehead with the blood that was on my hand.

I knelt there for what seemed like a very long time, and that's how the dream ended.

When I "awoke" the Holy Spirit revealed to me the meaning of the dream. The field represented America, a land of material goods in abundance. The magnificent eight-row combine represented the American society that is highly technological and sophisticated. The small boy represented the "little people" of society, especially the unborn. Society, in its desire for a great harvest (material greed) and in its blinding technology ran the boy over and didn't even know what it had done. The noise that blocked the warning and the dust that hid the child represent the confusion in our society. In America, even when a clear warning from God is sounded, it can't be heard because the confusion in our society is so great.

My wife and I coming to the aid of the boy represented the pro-life and Christian forces trying to aid the unborn and the "little people." God was there when I called and helped me to stop the bleeding. In this, the Spirit said that God is always with us to help us in our pro-life efforts. Then I called for the rescue squad. These are the other Christian and pro-life people that are needed to save the unborn. The significance of the gash in the throat being the only wound was that abortion was singled out by God as the worst and most deadly sin in our society. This sin strikes at the throat of our society, and if not stopped, it will mean sure death for us.

Even after the bleeding was stopped, the boy seemed to be in a very poor condition and looked near death. This represented the condition of our society which has rejected the laws of God and has become a culture of death.

The long time I knelt there waiting for help represented a long period of time in which Christian and pro-life forces will have to work and remain faithful to loving and serving the unborn until hopefully human life once again will be seen as a sacred gift from God.

It is significant that the dream ended with me kneeling there with no concrete solution to the problem. Right now, the future of the unborn and our society is in doubt and could go either way.

Finally, the Spirit showed me that the little boy is Jesus, our brother, who suffers and needs help.

Failed Attempts

At the time that God gave me this dream, Ann and I were already involved in some pro-life work. We had gone to the March for Life in Washington D.C., and we were active volunteers in the political campaigns of pro-life politicians. We had testified in local government hearings on behalf of pro-life organizations and against funding for Planned Parenthood and other pro-abortion organizations. We were caring for unwed mothers in our home and helping them to choose life.

But the message in that dream had a powerful impact upon me. I knew that I had to do something more to stop abortions. But what? I didn't know what to do, so I did the only thing that I thought would work. Every Saturday morning for the next two months I drove to the nearest abortion center which was about forty miles away in Dayton, Ohio. The abortionist usually did about twenty abortions each Saturday morning.

I would arrive early and stand outside the center. As the women approached the building I would talk to them and try to persuade them not to abort their baby. Many of them wouldn't stop to talk with me, but some did. I offered them help in every way I could, but my words fell on deaf ears.

One day a Volkswagen pulled up to the curb by the back entrance. The mother who was driving literally pushed her daughter out of the passenger side of the car and on to the sidewalk. Angry words were exchanged and then the car sped away.

I met the sixteen-year-old girl on the sidewalk and asked her if she was there for an abortion. She said yes. She was distraught and crying, and I got the impression that she didn't want to get an abortion. I explained to her about the life and development of her unborn child but she replied, "You don't understand mister, I have to get an abortion."

I told her that there was no law saying that she had to abort and that I would help her to give birth to her baby and that it wouldn't cost her anything. Once again she said, "You don't understand mister, I have to get an abortion. My parents are the kind that beat you up. If I come home pregnant they're going to beat the hell out of me."

As she cried about her plight I offered to take her home to my house if she wanted to live there until the baby was born. I knew that it would sound pretty weird for a complete stranger to offer shelter to a young girl, but I was desperate to save that baby. She said no to all of my offers and walked into the abortion center still crying. Another baby was murdered in the name of "choice".

The Devil sure came up with a clever lie when he inspired someone to call abortion "choice". That girl certainly felt that she had no choice in the matter. She was forced by her parents to abort or get beaten at home. I have come across many girls who were forced in one way or another to abort their babies.

Day after day, I stood outside the abortion center and talked to the women who approached. Once, one of the female assistants to the abortionist left the center to go to the adjacent convenience store to buy sodas for the staff. I walked along with her and pleaded that she stop killing the babies. I assured her that if she repented Jesus would forgive her.

She told me that she hated what she was doing and was planning to quit as soon as she could find a different job. I told her not to wait but to quit immediately. She was selling her soul for a minimum wage job while the abortionist was making about $7,000 each Saturday morning.

There were many times when the center's staffers would yell obscenities at me or tell me to go to Hell; they were filled with rage. When the abortionist arrived in his Mercedes, I would speak to him as he walked up the alley to the back door of his building. Repeatedly, I told him that God would forgive him if he would repent. He never spoke a word in reply but would silently enter the center to do his killing for money. For the abortionist, it's all about the money. They are paid assassins, nothing more.

One day a pregnant teenager and her older sister arrived in a car that had smoke pouring out from under the hood. I asked if I could be of assistance and tried to check out the problem, and they were grateful for my help. We looked under the hood and saw that the problem was a blown radiator hose. There was a gas station about fifty yards away so I borrowed a screwdriver, took off the old hose, and replaced it with a new one we purchased at the gas station.

During the whole time that I was fixing their car, I was trying to talk the girl out of her abortion. I worked slowly to give myself more time to persuade her, and I was hoping that she'd be so late for her appointment that they wouldn't take her. But all of my tactics failed and even though she was late, they rushed her through in less than thirty minutes. The staff was in a hurry to leave and one of them even had a hand on her back actually pushing the poor girl to walk faster out the back door. She was still stuffing her shirttail into her pants as she stood on the sidewalk. Her hair was a mess and she looked pale and about ready to pass out as her sister helped her into the car. It was so obvious that the abortionist and the staff didn't care about her at all. It was all about the money.

The Pregnancy Problem Center

All of my attempts to stop abortions outside the center failed. I was not able to change the mind of a single woman. It was heartbreaking and discouraging. I thought there had to be some other way. I knew that I needed to get to the women earlier because by the time they were at the door of the abortion center with the money in their pocket, they had already made up their minds.

I came up with the idea of opening an office that would offer free pregnancy tests while you wait. I reasoned that the moment a woman found out that she was pregnant, we would have a pro-life person to befriend her and to help her in any way she needed help. I was working on the assumption that women naturally love their babies and that they don't want to kill them. Women only resort to the unnatural violence of abortion when they feel cornered for some reason or when they are ignorant of what an abortion really does. I figured if a woman had friends she could count on to help her through the pregnancy, then many of them would never abort. Also, I knew that we would be able to educate a lot of women who didn't know about fetal development and who had been brainwashed by the abortionists into thinking that the unborn child is no different than an appendix. For years the abortionists have lied to women about the beginning of human life, and there are many women who really don't know that an abortion kills a living human being. If only women knew that fact, many would never abort.

I shared my thoughts with some friends from the prayer group. I was surprised to learn that my idea wasn't new but had already been put into practice by some people in larger cities. When I discovered that Cincinnati was the closest city with a crisis pregnancy center, I went there to visit and learn how to start a center myself.

The Cincinnati center was fantastic. They were serving lots of women in various ways and were saving many babies from being killed by abortion. They were very supportive of my desire to start a center in Sidney and gave me all of the information and advice they could. One of their leaders was a woman named Jackie who had thirteen children of her own. She had a wealth of knowledge and was a dynamo of activity. She volunteered to come to Sidney to help train the first volunteers if I would be able to get things started.

I approached two men in the Holy Angels prayer group with my idea of starting a crisis pregnancy help center. Ken and Mike were good pro-lifers and both agreed to work with me to start a center. It was going to take some money to rent office space and buy the necessary supplies. The three of us committed ten percent of our incomes to pay for expenses, enough to get us started.

We found a suitable building in downtown Sidney to rent. My dad was in charge of doing the carpentry work necessary to remodel the space for our needs. While the office was taking shape, I started to recruit female volunteers to work at the center. In a couple of weeks I had eighteen women from the Holy Angels prayer group and parish who were ready to start training. Jackie came from Cincinnati and did the training at my house during a couple of Saturdays. We opened our office on August 2, 1982, and we are still going strong as I write this in 2008. Of course there have been many changes at our center over the past twenty-five years. The history of the center would make an exciting book of its own that I'm not going to try to cover it here, but I will make a few comments.

We started quickly and learned a lot through experience. We had successes and failures, we laughed and we cried. We worked very hard, and many volunteers burned out. After three years of using only volunteers we hired a director which gave us more stability. Today we have several paid staff and dozens of volunteers. We have served tens of thousands of women and many babies have been saved from abortion. Allow me to recall a couple of life-saving stories from the early days.

Ann's Closet

A woman name Linda from a neighboring city called the center and said she couldn't come during regular business hours. My wife Ann set up an appointment with her for that evening to meet her at the center. Linda arrived with a female friend who was very large and muscular. Straightaway, Linda told Ann that she wanted an abortion. Ann explained that it was necessary to do a pregnancy test, which showed that Linda was indeed pregnant. Ann explained that our center did not do abortions and that we wanted to help her to carry her baby to term. Linda was angry because she thought our center did abortions, which was what she wanted. The woman she had brought with her was a lady wrestler, whom she had brought along for protection, in case the abortionist became a threat to her.

Ann kept talking with Linda and tried to draw out of her why she thought she wanted to abort her baby. It was tough going as Linda talked about one thing and then another. She was single and the relationship with the baby's father was over. She was worried about finances as well.

After about two hours of talking, Linda finally told Ann what was really bothering her. She didn't have any maternity clothes and felt embarrassed by her appearance. Ann knew just how to fix that problem. She told Linda and the lady wrestler to follow her to our home which was only four blocks away. Ann led them into our house and took them straight to our bedroom where she opened her clothes closet and told Linda to take whatever she wanted. Linda was overjoyed and picked out a number of maternity outfits. By the time she left our house all of her thoughts about abortion were gone, and she was looking forward to having her baby. About a year later she sent us a thank you letter with a picture of her beautiful little boy whom she named Joshua. It's amazing to think that the clothes in Ann's closet, and her willingness to give them away to a stranger, saved that little boy's life.

I'm Already a Mother

Cara was a sophomore at Bowling Green State University and was at home in Sidney for vacation. She came to our center for an abortion. When she stepped into our office she tried to hand the consultant three hundred dollars in cash and said, "I want an abortion." The consultant explained that it was our policy to do a pregnancy test to confirm pregnancy. The consultant had Cara watch a videotape on fetal development while she performed the test in the lab part of our office.

When the consultant returned with the test results she found Cara crying, the tears streaming down her cheeks. Cara stood up and embraced the consultant and said, "I can't have an abortion. I'm already a mother." By watching only ten minutes of a video she had come to realize that human life begins at conception and that the pre-born child in the uterus is a living, fully functioning human being no different that you or I.

It was amazing to me that a college sophomore didn't know the basic facts of human biology, but that was the case with Cara. As soon as she learned that abortion meant killing a baby, she was totally against it. She knew that giving birth would require a lot of courage and that she would have to make some changes in her plans for her future, but she had the help and resources of our center to help her along the way. With our help she carried the baby to term and delivered a beautiful baby girl.

Education is so important in the pro-life battle. When women know the facts about life and about abortion, they will naturally want to choose life. And if they have the support of friends and the necessary resources, they usually will choose life. We have seen this happen at our center many, many times.

My Friend, what are you doing to be pro-life and to save babies from the cruel death of abortion? Are you praying? Fasting? Voting pro-life? May God have mercy on the souls of politicians who support legalized abortion and those people who vote for them for they are doing the devil's bidding.

Are you helping your local crises pregnancy center in some way? Financially? Volunteering? There are many ways that volunteers can be of help to their local center. I hope you will look up your local center in the yellow pages and call them today to see how you can help.

A word of warning. To do nothing in the face of so great an evil is to endanger your soul to eternal damnation. That may sound excessively harsh to you, but I believe it is the truth and if you really saw abortion the way God sees it I'm sure you would agree with me. Abortion is the great moral evil of our time that is leading millions to physical and spiritual death. Jesus said, *"The thief (the*

Devil) comes to kill, steal, and destroy." That is a perfect description of abortion, which is the work of the Devil.

Jesus also said, "*I have come that you may have life abundantly.*" My friend, if you want to be on the side of Jesus you must be on the side of life and you must work to defend life and protect life in all of its stages, from conception until natural death. Today we face attacks against life from many different groups and various technologies. Pope John Paul II has said that we are living in a culture of death and that it is imperative that we build a culture of life.

Build a culture of life in your own life, marriage, and family. Let the greed, self-centeredness, and materialism of modern society give way to a society that is generous, self-sacrificing, and trusting in God. Faithful Catholics who are living examples of Christ's love in our world (in short, saints) are desperately needed to light mankind's path and to lead us out of the darkness of the culture of death in which we are ensnared. Without such saints to illuminate our society we shall surely be lost.

You may protest and say, "I can't do it, I can't be a saint!" And I say, "You can, because sanctity doesn't depend on you but upon God!" A saint is just a sinner who looks into the face of Jesus and sees Infinite Mercy. A saint is just a sinner who embraces Jesus and feels his Sacred Heart beating with love for himself. A saint is just a sinner who repentantly kneels at the feet of Jesus and feels His hands upon his head imparting forgiveness, healing, and the Holy Spirit. A saint is just a sinner who walks with Jesus, filled with the power of the Holy Spirit to do the will of Jesus in all things. Yes, my Friend, you can be a saint, and God needs you to be a saint in this culture of death in which we live. This evil generation seeks a sign and the sign that God will give to this world is the holiness of our lives as we follow Christ who came to give life abundantly. Please surrender yourself completely to Jesus and by doing so, you will become a source of abundant life to many others. God the Holy Spirit will guide you and lead you into some sort of service in the pro-life movement as you offer yourself. The pro-life movement is God's work and He will certainly use you in some way.

Lost Lives

As you serve God in the pro-life movement you must be prepared to suffer setbacks. Along with the joy of saving lives at our women's center, we have suffered the heartbreak of losing babies to abortion.

I remember Tamara, a pregnant fifteen-year-old girl who came to our center. She was a babysitter for a family with a couple of small children. The father of those kids had forced Tamara into having sex with him, and she had come to us for help. Her dad was a minister, and she felt ashamed and didn't want to tell him about her pregnancy. She wouldn't go to the police and wouldn't tell us who the man who raped her was.

After a lot of persuasion she agreed to tell her dad at our office the next Saturday morning. We thought that her parents would be supportive if only they knew what was happening. That was our plan when she left our office on Tuesday.

Wednesday afternoon my phone rang at home. I had given Tamara my home phone number in case she needed help. It was Tamara crying on the phone. She told me that she had just gotten home from Dayton where she had had an abortion. My heart sank and I asked what had happened to our plan.

She explained that the man that she babysat for had waited until her parents had left for work and then came to her house. He told her that she had to get into his car and that he was taking her to Dayton for an abortion. She told me that she wasn't able to stop him and cried all the way there and back. She never would tell us the man's identity because she was afraid of him. From that point on, all of our efforts with Tamara centered on trying to help her find healing in all the ways that she needed it. She was a victim in so many ways. Legal abortion in this country makes it possible for this kind of tragedy to be repeated in the lives of millions of people.

Sandy was another teenager who came to us for a pregnancy test which turned out to be positive. When Sandy told her mother she flew into a rage. Screaming obscenities she hit Sandy repeatedly. Later she suddenly burst into Sandy's room as Sandy lay on the bed. She pounced on top of Sandy and began to ram her knee into Sandy's abdomen in an attempt to make her miscarry the baby.

Sandy was able to escape and walked to our center. I went to the center, picked up Sandy, and brought her to my house. Ann and I promised to protect her as best as we could. Soon we got a tip that the mother had called the police, who would be coming to my house to look for her. We didn't want her to be taken back to her abusive mother who had given her a bruised eye, a swollen jaw, and had tried to kill her baby. So Sandy got into my car, and we drove around the countryside for several hours thinking about what we could do to protect her.

Later that evening I called home to check out the situation. Ann told me that the police were looking for us, and that if I didn't bring her to the police station, they would charge me with kidnapping. I didn't know what else I could do so I took Sandy to the police station and explained everything that had happened. I demanded that they call children's services in order to protect Sandy from her mother.

Late that evening someone from children's services came to the police station and interviewed Sandy and examined her injuries. They concluded that they were going to take her back home. When I protested that there was a good chance that she would suffer more violence there and that she should instead be put into protective custody, I was warned to stay out of their business and be grateful that I wasn't charged with kidnapping. They "assured" me that Sandy would be safe and that they would send a counselor to the house the next morning.

I was furious that they cared so little for Sandy's safety! They were taking her right back to the place where she had been beaten earlier in the day. But there was nothing I could do about it. Later, when I inquired about Sandy, the authorities refused to give me any information about her. I never did find out what happened to her and her baby. Sometimes pro-life work is very frustrating.

Ann's Arrest

During the summer of 1989 there was a pro-life initiative called "Operation Rescue" going on all across America. Ann and I were in touch with some other pro-lifers who were planning to do a rescue at the abortion center in Dayton, Ohio.

A rescue consisted of a group of pro-lifers who would block the doors of an abortion center with their bodies thus preventing anyone from entering and thereby getting an abortion. Other pro-lifers would speak with women as they arrived for their abortion and try to persuade them to choose life. The abortionist would call the police who would arrest the pro-lifers for trespassing, but the whole process would take several hours and hopefully some babies would be saved.

The rescue was planned for a Saturday morning in June when the abortion center would have many appointments. Ann and I discussed who would take part in the rescue and get arrested. Since we had five small children of our own at that time we knew that one of us had to stay out of jail in order to take care of the kids. Even though Ann was six months along in her pregnancy, she was determined to be a part of the rescue. We decided that she would help block the doors and that I would stay on the sidewalk with the kids.

We had twenty-three pro-lifers who were committed to blocking the doors with their bodies. Just before the staff of the abortion center arrived, the pro-lifers sat down in front of the doors which made it impossible for anyone to enter the building. When the abortionist and the staff arrived they were very angry and demanded that the pro-lifers leave.

The police were called. When they arrived they quickly determined that this was an act of civil disobedience similar to other rescues that were being staged all over the nation that summer. The police spoke with the pro-lifers and tried to negotiate with them. Our leaders tried to keep the negotiating phase going as long as possible in order to delay the arrests and keep the abortion center closed all morning. Every minute we could keep those doors closed was important because women would be arriving all through the morning for their abortions, and we needed a chance to talk with them.

When the police determined that they were going to arrest the pro-lifers in order to remove them, they called for more officers and a police bus for transport. All of the police logistics took quite a long time and in order to slow the arrest process even more, the pro-lifers were completely passive and let their bodies go limp when they were arrested. This tactic meant that the police would have to carry each pro-lifer to the bus which took up more time. Because Ann was six months pregnant (with our sixth child, Maggie, who was born on Respect Life Sunday that October 1st) she decided to walk to the police bus instead of being carried. The officer who arrested Ann was a nice guy and actually apologized for having to do his duty because he was also pro-life. Some of the other officers who were pro-abortion were very mean and mistreated some of the pro-lifers.

The whole rescue lasted several hours and completely disrupted their killing business. Not one woman was able to enter and have an abortion that day. During the rescue about thirty women arrived for their abortions, and the sidewalk counselors spoke with all of them. One woman went with our counselor to a nearby crises pregnancy center and with their help she decided to choose life for her baby and not to have an abortion. But that wasn't the only baby saved that day. As it turned out there was a pregnant woman in jail who was planning to abort her baby and some pro-lifers were put in the same jail cell with her. The pro-lifers were able to persuade her not to abort, but to give birth. That made at least two babies that our rescue saved, and who knows what effect the rescue had on the other women.

Ann spent twenty-four hours in jail before I was able to get her out on bail ($1,014 in exact change--really, I'm not kidding—I brought a thousand and twenty dollars and they wouldn't break the twenty dollar bill). The jail time was pretty tough on her because it was very hot, over 100 degrees in her cell, and she was six months pregnant, but she offered all her suffering up to the Lord.

Ann was charged with trespassing. At her hearing the judge said that she would not be allowed to defend herself by saying that she trespassed in order to save someone's life. If she tried to use that as her defense she would be held in contempt of court. In fact, the judge gave us a whole list of words that were forbidden for us to use in our defense or we would be charged with contempt of court. Some of the words were: baby, life, God, abortion, murder, rescue, and many others which made her defense impossible.

So Ann pleaded guilty and was fined $250.00, given a thirty-day suspended jail sentence, and put on probation for one year. Now she felt like a real Christian. After all, the Apostles all spent time in jail for the sake of the Gospel. Now Ann was a jail bird too, although a much prettier one than the Apostles!

Not long after Ann's arrest, Operation Rescue was effectively stopped by a federal court which declared that rescuers were involved in "organized crime," which violated federal racketeering laws that carried penalties of more than twenty years in prison and million-dollar fines. Faced with such enormous penalties, pro-lifers had to find new ways of protecting the innocent unborn children.

Amazing Grace

Sometimes in life you may be tempted to discouragement because it looks like all your efforts have not changed a thing. We must be careful not to fall into that trap. Our efforts always change ourselves, if nothing else. We grow in virtue every time we make an effort to please God and do the right thing.

Many times our efforts and prayers are having a good result, but we aren't aware of it for one reason or another. Other times it just takes time for our efforts to reach a critical mass before the desired change occurs. That was the case with the abortionist at the center where we rescued.

Lots of people prayed and fasted for his conversion. Many efforts were made to shut down his center. I used to tell him repeatedly that if he would repent, then God would forgive him. Finally, one day it happened!

He was invited by some of his friends to go on a Christian retreat. During the retreat he gave his life to Christ and experienced a conversion. The light of Christ illuminated his thinking. He soon realized that abortion was wrong and that he could not continue to do them. He closed the abortion center! Praise the Lord!

Not long after that he made an appearance at the Miami County Right to Life Society's monthly meeting. I heard that he was going to speak and attended the meeting. He addressed the group and told us about his conversion and his new relationship with Jesus. He said that he was sorry for the evil that he had done and that he would provide pre-natal care free of charge for women who were indigent. When he finished I embraced him as a brother in Christ and so did everyone else. This was what we had hoped and prayed for, and now it was a reality.

Part VII
The Voice of Christ

Wolves Among Us

Jesus gave to the Apostles everything that was necessary to get to heaven. The Apostles, in turn, handed on to their hearers the Sacred Tradition that they had received from Jesus. This Sacred Tradition, or Deposit of Faith, contains everything that we need today to get to Heaven.

Anyone who claims that they have a new revelation from God which must be followed to attain salvation is a false teacher. Many false teachers have declared new revelations over the past twenty centuries and have led many people astray from the true Faith, founded upon the Apostles.

I've spent most of my adult life trying to pass on to the next generation the Sacred Deposit of Faith that was given to the Church by the Apostles. As a religion teacher in a Catholic school, I've tried my best to teach the faith accurately according to the mind of the Church.

In order to learn the faith, I've done a lot of reading, especially the writings of Saints. My wife Ann likes to say that all of her spiritual directors are "dead and canonized," and I have come to agree wholeheartedly with her. There are no better teachers of the faith than those who have passed the test of time and holiness.

But, even today, God continues to raise up teachers and preachers who inspire us towards holiness. One of my favorite inspirational speakers was the late Archbishop Fulton J. Sheen who kept his audiences spellbound while he taught the truths of the Catholic Faith. I've spent many wonderful hours listening to his sermons on audio tapes while working or walking.

Another of my contemporary favorites is Father John Corapi who speaks boldly and fearlessly to our modern society. After his amazing conversion, God has used him in a powerful way to help reform the American Catholic Church.

Archbishop Sheen and Father Corapi are just two of the many wonderful Catholic teachers who have faithfully passed on the true Faith during my lifetime. But not all who claim to speak for the Church have done so faithfully. There are many "wolves in sheep's clothing," as Father Corapi is fond of saying. These are priests, religious, and teachers in Catholic institutions who are not faithful to the Sacred Tradition of the Church and who teach their own erroneous opinions to the detriment of their listeners. Sadly, there are many such wolves among us who do not spare the flock but instead devour them with their false teachings. I have encountered many such false teachers during my years of involvement in Catholic education. I want to share with you a few stories so that you will be better able to recognize these wolves and steer your life away from them. .

There was the pre-cana course that Ann and I were required to take before our wedding. We went to an "Engaged Encounter" weekend retreat at a retreat house in

Dayton. The format called for ten-minute talks on various topics given by a married couple and then each engaged couple would spend about forty-five minutes alone, dialoguing about the topic. The intended result was that the engaged couple would learn how to discuss substantive issues and come to a much better understanding of each other. It's not a bad format if it's done properly, but ours was an absolute disaster.

On Saturday evening the leadership panel consisted of two married couples and one priest. Fr. Tim introduced the topic of Catholic sexual morality by telling two sexually obscene jokes. Mike and Cathy then gave a short ten-minute speech on sexuality that was jam-packed with as much evil as can be imagined.

They stated that like most young dating couples they had had a strong sexual attraction for each other when they were dating. They said that they "prayed about having premarital sex and that the Lord said it was okay for them" and so they did. They advised the sixty-six engaged couples on that retreat to "pray about it." If you think pre-marital sex is okay for you, then go ahead.

When Mike made that statement I was so angry that I could hardly see straight. I wanted to scream, "Don't listen to him!" I wonder how many of those couples were working hard to stay sexually pure and trying to hang on to their virginity. Then they had the rug pulled out from under their feet at a required Catholic marriage preparation class by a guy who told them that fornication was okay if you "prayed about it." Sadly, Mike was just getting started.

Next he told us that contraception was definitely okay, and that we didn't need to even "pray about it". He mentioned that the official teaching of the Church was against contraception and that Pope Paul VI had condemned it in an encyclical, but then he laughed out loud and said, "But nobody listens to him!" Then he proceeded to describe the various types of contraception that he and his wife had used and finished by telling us that the birth control pill was "by far the best method." Then the couples were sent away to dialogue about the topic.

Well, I was going to have a little dialogue with Fr. Tim and Mike. I went to my room to get my Bible and went searching for them. I found them in a hallway and confronted them. First, I told Father Tim that he was very wrong in telling sex jokes. I showed him in Scripture where St. Paul taught, *"Let nothing suggestive or obscene pass your lips because your holiness forbids it."* Fr. Tim hung his head in shame and said that I was right and that he wouldn't do it again. That was great, but now it was Mike's turn.

I showed him in Scripture where Jesus said, *"Fornicators shall not inherit the Kingdom of God,"* and I demanded that he retract in the next session what he had taught. His response blew my mind.

He replied, "You can't go by that book (the Bible); it's two-thousand years old and out-dated! Don't you read Time Magazine? It tells us that today's sociologists think that pre-marital sex is healthy for a relationship." His reply revealed how hopelessly brainwashed he was by modernism.

I turned to Fr. Tim and asked, "Did you hear that hogwash?" Fr. Tim told Mike that he was wrong and that fornication and contraception were mortal sins. Mike got angry and walked away. Then I demanded that Fr. Tim make a retraction and present the correct Church teaching during the next session. He flatly refused saying "He said it, I didn't." I responded, "Yes, but you're a priest and you sat right next to him and didn't say a word. Your silence was seen as approval by all of those couples."

Once again he refused to make the correction so I informed him that Ann and I would leave the retreat immediately. We collected our things and "shook the dust from our feet" on the front steps as we left. The next day we informed the pastor of our parish about all of this, and then the three of us composed a letter to the Archbishop to inform him of the situation. We never found out if any action was taken to rectify that scandalous situation.

More Whoppers

At one point, I took courses for two years in preparation to become a permanent deacon. Some teachers were fine, but some others were totally out in left field. I had one teacher who claimed that there were no differences between men and woman – none, not even physical or anatomical! I pressed her, on this issue but she wouldn't admit to any differences.

Then there was the priest who would pound his fist on his desk while yelling, "The Pope is wrong! The Pope is wrong and I'm right!" The topic was the Sacrament of

Reconciliation and the teaching of Pope John Paul II was at odds with his teaching so in his mind the Pope must be wrong. His arrogance and pridefulness were truly breathtaking.

There was another priest who taught us that adultery was sometimes morally good. He said that usually adultery was a sin, but that sometimes it can be used in a morally good way to "spice up marriage". He even said that sometimes it's the *best thing a person can do for the marriage*. You're probably saying that you can't believe a priest would teach that way, but it's true. Another student and I talked to him after class just to make sure that we hadn't misunderstood him in some way. He clearly reiterated that there are no intrinsically evil actions of any kind and that sometimes adultery was a moral good.

A different priest taught us that we don't have any certainty about anything that Jesus said or did. For him, the Gospel accounts may or may not have occurred. When I pointed out to him that the Second Vatican Council document *Dei Verbum* stated that the four Gospels are of "historical character" and tell us what "Jesus really did and taught," he became angry and said that he would not call on me anymore. Wow! The champion of academic freedom sure didn't allow any freedom in his class!

Then there was the professor who stated that there was no bodily resurrection of Jesus but that only His memory lives on in our hearts and minds in a very profound way. A few of the men in the class actually had their faith somewhat shaken by her statements until I was able to bring them back to their senses.

Volcanic Eruptions

Finally, the one who takes the grand prize in my mind, was a Scripture professor who was much more of a radical feminist than a Catholic. Everything in life was a feminist issue for her. It was painful to have to sit and listen to her insane ranting and hate-filled diatribes against men.

She started one class by asking, "What do you think of the image of Jesus as the Good Shepherd?" I thought I knew where she would take this topic so I quickly replied that I loved it and thought of it as a fitting description of Jesus. A couple of the others students chimed in with similar comments. It was more than she could take.

She exploded with, "Well, I hate it! If Jesus is the Good Shepherd then that makes me a sheep--- and I'm nobody's damn sheep! Besides that, He never said it. That statement was written by men who wanted to establish a patriarchal Church to oppress women and keep them in subjugation. So they put those words into the mouth of Jesus as a means to help establish a patriarchal mentality!" Her hatred spewed forth like a volcano.

I have seen similarities in all of the heretical teachers I've encountered. Arrogance, pride, and a complete disdain for Church authority dominated each one's personality. They were all certain that they were right and the Church was wrong. They all had an agenda, some issue that they were bound and determined to push down the throats of their listeners. In pushing their agenda, the truth was often the first casualty. They tended to be hedonistic and had no regard for discipline or rules. Later I found out that one priest (the one who said adultery was okay) had quit the priesthood and run off with a woman, and another priest was defrocked for molesting children.

My Friend, as you draw closer to Christ you should also draw closer to His Church because the Church is the Body of Christ. If your spirituality is leading you away from the Catholic Church, then it is not a true spirituality but a counterfeit.

Today there are thousands of competing theologies and spiritualities all claiming to be correct. But Jesus established only one Church and that Church is the Catholic Church governed by the Pope who is the successor of St. Peter. It was to St. Peter and his successors that Jesus made the promise, *"Whatever you bind on earth shall be bound in Heaven and whatever you loose on earth shall be loosed in Heaven."* Jesus knew that He would guide the Popes and the Church through the Holy Spirit so that they would give correct teaching and guidance to His followers. Don't allow false teachers either inside or outside of the Church to lead you astray from the true Deposit of Faith found in it's fullness in the doctrines and practices of the Catholic Church.

The doctrines of the Catholic Church are correct. The Church's teachings on faith and morals are authoritative and require our assent because they are inspired by the Holy Spirit. It is only logical that Jesus would leave a living, human authority on this earth to speak for Him. Otherwise, how could we be certain that what we believe is true? The Magisterium of the Catholic Church, composed of the Pope and those Bishops in union with him, is that living voice of Christ on earth today to be our sure guide in matters pertaining to our salvation.

A place where the living voice of Christ can be heard clearly today is in the *Catechism of the Catholic Church*. Pope John Paul II ordered that this book be compiled for the express purpose of clearing up the confusion that ensued after the Second Vatican Council. He declared that the Catechism provided a "sure norm" that the faithful could trust as authentic teaching. The *Catechism of the Catholic Church* has been a tremendous gift for our time, and I urge everyone to become very familiar with it.

Some people think that they only need the Bible as their guide in religious matters, but that belief can't possibly be correct. Think about it. Where did the list of New Testament books come from? There was not a consensus in the early Church as to an exact list. Near the end of the fourth century the Magisterium of the Catholic Church defined the twenty-seven book list of the New Testament. Only then could the faithful have certainty that each of those twenty-seven books contained the Word of God.

If someone claims that the Magisterium of the Catholic Church is not infallible, then they cannot claim the New Testament is the Word of God. After all, if the Magisterium can make errors in matters of faith and morals, then it is possible that they erred when defining the New Testament list of books. Maybe there are books on the list that aren't really God's Word and therefore can't be trusted. Logically, you can only claim an infallible New Testament if you also claim an infallible Magisterium that defined the contents of the New Testament. You can't have one without the other. St. Augustine clearly saw this when he wrote, "I only believe in the Gospels because the Church tells me to."

With further thought, it is easy to conclude that it was necessary for Jesus to leave a living, human authority on earth to infallibly interpret the meaning of Sacred Scripture and apply it correctly to contemporary situations. If there were no infallible earthly authority to speak for Christ, then people would argue endlessly over the correct understanding of Sacred Scripture and over the correct application of God's word to modern circumstances. There would be no way of settling these arguments without a divine authority on earth and people would endlessly split into like-minded groups. That is precisely what has occurred among Protestants over the last five centuries because they don't have an infallible Magisterium.

The infallible guidance of the Magisterium is a great, great gift from God to us. Through it we have a sure guide to lead us as we journey through life to our goal of Heaven. If you were lost in the wilderness and somehow a local native came along to guide you to safety, you would be very grateful. God, in His mercy and love for us, wants all of us to gain eternal life and has graciously provided an earthly guide to lead us home. Don't allow pridefulness to cause you to reject this guide that God has provided as so many have in the past. I fear that many souls have been lost to Hell forever through their prideful rejection of the authority of the Magisterium. Their attitude of "I'll do it my way!" led to their eternal damnation. If there's a theme song in Hell, I'll bet it's the old Frank Sinatra hit, "I Did It My Way."

The true follower of Christ has the attitude, "*Not my will but Thy will be done.*" That was the attitude of Jesus as He faced His fearful passion. It must be ours, too, as we journey through this life. We must always submit our thoughts and will to the will of God as presented to us through the Church, remembering the words of Jesus to the Apostles who were the original Magisterium, "*Whoever hears you, hears Me, and whoever rejects you, rejects Me.*"

What should you do when the teaching of the Church conflicts with your thoughts on some matter of faith or morals? You should re-examine both the Church's teaching and your own attitude. Often, people misunderstand what the Church actually teaches, and this misunderstanding deforms the teaching and makes it unacceptable. A person should consult the *Catechism of the Catholic Church* or visit a faithful Catholic website in order to truly understand the what and the why of the Church's teaching.

If a conflict still persists after you actually know and understand the Church's teaching, then you need to examine your own attitude on the topic. You need to be brutally honest with yourself and question yourself about why you think the way you do. Many opinions are formed from inadequate or inaccurate information. We are masters of rationalizing our behaviors in order to avoid the demands of holiness. The narrow path of Christ seems too narrow for us, and so we justify taking an easier, alternate route. This kind of rationalization is the path to Hell, and you don't want that to be your destination. The sure and safe path to Heaven is to form your conscience according to the teachings of the Church. Then, by the grace of God, follow your rightly-formed conscience in all of your activities, and if you fail, seek the mercy of God which is always there for you. It is far better to endeavor to follow the truth and fail occasionally (or often), than to follow a lie and succeed.

I take such comfort in knowing that the Catholic Church is the highest spiritual authority on earth and speaks with the voice of Christ. As long as I try to follow the guidance of the Church in every spiritual matter, I know that I am safe in the heart of Jesus. My Friend, I want you to experience the joy and security that comes from faithful obedience to the Catholic Church. Give yourself completely to Jesus and to His Church that He established for your spiritual nourishment and protection. Then your life will be filled with the joy of the Lord and will bear abundant fruit for the Kingdom of God.

Heart Attack

May 20, 1994, was field day at Lehman High School. Throughout the day the students and faculty enjoyed all kinds of sporting competitions, both indoors and outdoors. I played a singles tennis match against the best player on the boys team and got annihilated 6-1, 6-0, in two sets. Right after the tennis massacre, I took my turn on the dunk the clown, or in this case, dunk the teacher machine. I had volunteered to be a victim in order to help the student council raise money for a charitable cause. Repeatedly, I fell into some very cold water as a baseball struck the trigger mechanism, much to the delight of the students.

When my turn on the dunking machine was over I went into the school to dry off and change clothes. At that time I noticed a feeling of nausea but didn't think much of it. When school dismissed an hour later I took some religious videos back to the Catholic lending library. By that time I was feeling weak and my chest and left arm had begun to ache. I chalked it up to overexertion in the tennis match even though the librarian suggested that I go to the hospital. I didn't think that I was a likely candidate for a heart attack. I was only forty years old and in good physical condition. I didn't smoke or drink, and there was no history of heart disease in my family.

Since I felt tired, I decided to rest for a while by watching a high school baseball game. When the game was over I felt better and went home. I mentioned to Ann how rotten I had felt but didn't realize that I had just sat through a mild heart attack.

During the next two weeks I felt unusually tired, but I thought the fatigue was from all of the end-of-the-school-year work and activities. June 3, 1994, was my wife's forty-first birthday so we took the whole family to Pizza Hut to celebrate. After the meal I had some heartburn but thought the pizza caused it. We then did some grocery shopping and went home.

I was doing a little work in the garage when a deep burning pain developed in my chest. I went into the house and told Ann about it and ate a popsicle to try to cool myself down. Ann wanted me to go to the hospital. She had an uncle who died of a heart attack when he was forty, and she didn't want that to happen to me. I told her that I had to take our daughter Maria to a teen-age pageant in Columbus the next morning and that if I went to the hospital they would keep me overnight for observation and ruin our plans. Plus, it would probably cost us a thousand dollars, which we didn't have.

Her next thought was a stroke of genius. She suggested that we take the twenty-minute drive to the hospital and just sit in the parking lot. If I started feeling better, we would go home, not costing us anything. If I got worse, we would be at the hospital and could get treatment. With nothing to lose I quickly agreed and off we went to the hospital.

By the time we arrived, I was in severe pain and immediately entered the emergency room. I walked past the registration desk and told the staff that my chest was killing me. I laid down on the nearest table. The emergency room personnel flew into action and as quickly as possible determined that it was indeed a heart attack. They put an I.V. in each arm, and there were tubes and wires everywhere. They gave me a shot of medicine to break up the clot in my heart and gave me morphine for the pain.

As I lay flat on my back a nurse spoke kindly to me and tried to reassure me that I would be okay. I propped myself up on one elbow so that I could speak to her up close and personally. I told her, "I know I'm going to be okay. Whether I live or die I'm going to be okay. I took care of that years ago when I gave my life to Christ." It was my sincere hope at that moment to make a deep impression upon her and hopefully lead one more soul to Jesus before I died. I thought if she saw a man on death's door and he had no fear of dying due to his faith in Jesus, it might help her to entrust her life to Christ. I had no idea if she was a Christian or not, but I wanted to help her believe.

Other than that moment, my time in the emergency room and in the intensive care unit has been erased from my memory. The next day I was transferred to a bigger hospital in Dayton where I underwent angioplasty to open up an artery.

The heart attack had been severe but not fatal. It was certainly a shock to everyone and created a tremendous outpouring of love and support from family and friends. I began a new heart healthy regimen of diet, exercise, rest, and medicine that has kept me reasonably healthy and able to lead a normal life for the past thirteen years.

A number of people who came to visit me after my heart attack made comments like, "I can't believe that God would let you have a heart attack. After all, you're such a religious man and you teach the Faith and you work so hard for the pro-life movement." I appreciated their kind words, but I had to respond in a way that would correct their thinking.

I told them that just because a person loves and serves God that doesn't exempt him from hardships and trials. Everybody has to carry their own cross and follow in Jesus' footsteps. It is in suffering that God teaches us the most powerful and enduring lessons of life. It was through suffering that Jesus saved the world, and through our suffering we can play a part in the world's redemption. St. Paul wrote, *"I fill up in my own flesh what is lacking in the sufferings of Christ on behalf of His Body, the Church."* St. Paul saw his suffering as a participation in the suffering that Jesus endured to redeem the world.

It is so important that we have a correct view of suffering and understand its value. Any kind of suffering is a unique opportunity for us to grow in grace and virtue. We can join our suffering to Jesus' and in that way our suffering becomes redemptive. In the lives of many saints there are many stories of how they suffered patiently for the conversion of sinners.

We all suffer in various ways and for various reasons and to various degrees. Some saints are even known as "victim souls" because of the extreme sufferings they endured. Only in Heaven will we know the tremendous value of what they suffered and how many souls found the grace of conversion because of it. The key to making suffering redemptive lies in our attitude and will.

If we freely offer up our suffering to God in a spirit of love for Him and desiring Him to use us as an instrument of His grace, then our suffering becomes a means of expiation for our own sins and a channel of grace to others. So much suffering in our world is wasted because people do not offer it to God. They don't realize the spiritual value that it could have for themselves and others. What could be a means of sanctification for the spiritual value of many is thrown away because it is not given to God.

The best way to offer up our sufferings to God is to unite them with Jesus on the cross at Mass. Every Mass is a re-presentation of the once-for-all sacrifice of Jesus on the cross. As the priest offers the bread and wine we should offer ourselves completely to God. We should offer our heart, mind, will, body, time, talents, and our sufferings to God. When the bread and wine are consecrated into the Body and Blood of Jesus, then every part of our lives is also consecrated. As the Body and Blood of Jesus is offered on the altar to the Eternal Father, our lives, too, are offered in union with Him and everything in our lives takes on a sacred quality.

My Friend, please don't waste your sufferings. Offer them up to God and use them as a means of salvation for yourself and the whole world. When hardship comes your way, don't get angry and question God's love for you. Instead, put complete trust in Jesus, knowing that He only allows evil to happen in order to bring a greater good from it. He allows us to suffer so that we and others might benefit from it.

Conclusion

"Now Jesus did many other signs in the presence of His disciples that are not written in this book. But these are written that you may come to believe that Jesus is the Messiah, the Son of God, and that through this belief you may have life in His name." These words of St. John express my own thoughts as I bring this book to its end.

I could write dozens of more stories of God's actions in my life during the past thirty years and I hope to do so in the future. But the stories that I have shared with you in this book have had a profound effect upon me, and I hope they have touched your heart in some way.

Faith in Jesus is really a matter of the heart. I like to often substitute the word "trust" for the word "faith." To put faith in someone means to put your trust in them and to have faith in Jesus means to trust Him with your life. Many of us have trusted someone only to have our trust betrayed, hurting us deeply. That will not be the case with Jesus. He will never betray your trust. He proved that by dying on the cross for you. Your heart is safe with Him.

His love for you is perfect and He calls you into His own heart. His heart is on fire with love for you and for all mankind. Please respond to His love by entrusting your heart to Him. That is the first step in any spiritual growth.

I have prepared for you a spiritual "game plan" to help you grow in the Spirit everyday. I've called it "My Path to Heaven," and if you follow this game plan it will be of great spiritual benefit to you. It will help you keep your heart centered on God and your life moving in the right direction.

Part VIII
Spiritual Game Plan

My Path to Heaven

Someone asked Him, *"Lord, will only a few people be saved?"* He answered them, *"**Strive** to enter through the narrow gate, for many, I tell you, will attempt to enter but will not be strong enough."* Our Divine Savior tells us to *strive* to enter. The dictionary defines *strive* as to try hard; work hard; struggle. A person does not accidentally end up in Heaven! The path is narrow and rough, and a person must strive to enter. Our strength comes from the Lord so we must pray daily and use all the sacramental and spiritual help available. The following is a sure-fire spiritual game plan that will help you achieve your goal of Heaven, but it only works if you actually follow it with all of your heart.

Daily

You shall love the Lord your God with all your heart, and all your mind, and all your strength.

1. Receive Holy Communion if possible
2. Read some Sacred Scripture
3. Pray the Rosary
4. Personal Prayer Time
5. Wear your Scapular

6. Spiritual reading, especially from saints
7. Fulfill indulgences for yourself

You shall love your neighbor as yourself.
1. Be of service to others
2. Be generous with your time, talents, and treasures
3. Practice sexual purity
4. Give the Faith to others
5. Pray for the souls in Purgatory and gain indulgences for them
6. Practice humility and poverty according to your state in life
7. Obey the laws of God and the Church

Weekly

1. Participate in Sunday Mass

    As a Catholic, you have a serious obligation to participate at Sunday Mass (or Saturday evening). To intentionally skip Sunday Mass without a sufficiently serious reason would be a mortal sin.
2. Perform penance or prayer every Friday.

    As a Catholic, you have a serious obligation to do penance every Friday. During Lent, you must abstain from meat on Fridays, but during the rest of the year, you can substitute some other form of penance or perform some act of piety or prayer. I suggest that you pray The Chaplet of Devine Mercy every Friday. It is a perfect prayer to help you focus on the passion of our Lord Jesus Christ.

My Gospel

Monthly

1. Go to Confession as often as needed, but everyone would benefit from Confession *at least once a month*
2. Perform First Friday Devotion
3. Perform First Saturday Devotion

First Friday Devotion

History

The desire for a First Friday Devotion was revealed by Jesus to St. Margaret Mary Alacoque in a series of visions in 1675 in France. He showed her His heart on fire with love for mankind, a love that unfortunately was often ignored or treated with contempt. He asked her to make up for this coldness and ingratitude by receiving Holy Communion as often as she was allowed, and particularly on the first Friday of each month, and to spread this devotion to others.

Purposes

To establish devotion to the Sacred Heart of Jesus and to make reparation for the sins of the world which wound that most loving heart.

Practices

1. Receive Holy Communion validly and worthily, that is not being in a state of mortal sin, on nine consecutive first Fridays of the month
2. In addition the communicant must have intention of making reparation to the Sacred Heart of Jesus for all the sinfulness and ingratitude of mankind.

Promises

"I promise you, in the excess of the mercy of My Heart, that Its all-powerful love will grant to all those who shall receive Communion on the first Friday of nine consecutive months the grace of final repentance; they shall not die under My displeasure nor without receiving the Sacraments, My Divine Heart becoming their assured refuge at that last hour."

First Saturday Devotion

History

The desire for a First Saturday Devotion was revealed by the Blessed Virgin Mary to the three children at Fatima in 1917. On December 10, 1925, the Virgin revealed more details about the devotion to Sister Lucia, the only seer still alive and at that time a cloistered nun. From that time, the devotion has spread throughout the world on the day (Saturday) that the Church has traditionally honored the Blessed Virgin.

Purposes

To establish devotion (in accordance with God's wishes) to the Immaculate Heart of Mary, and to make reparation for sins against God's mother.

Practices

The devotion involves the following practices on five consecutive first Saturdays with the specific intention of making reparation for offenses against the Blessed Virgin Mary.

1. Go to Confession (within 8 days before or after the first Saturday)
2. Receive Holy Communion
3. Recite five decades of the Rosary
4. "Keep me company for fifteen minutes while meditating on fifteen mysteries of the Rosary" (separate from the Rosary itself)

Promises

1. The Virgin Mary's assistance at the hour of death with the graces necessary for salvation for those who practice the devotion.
2. Salvation of souls and peace as a result of promoting the Devotion to the Immaculate Heart of Mary

Annually

1. You must participate at Mass on Holy Days of Obligation. In America they are:
   - Christmas, December 25
   - Mary, The Mother of God, January 1
   - Ascension of the Lord (date varies)
   - The Assumption of Mary, August 15
   - All Saints, November 1
   - The Immaculate Conception of the Blessed Virgin Mary, December 8
2. Obey church laws on fasting and abstinence during Lent. Catholics age 18-59 must fast on Ash Wednesday and Good Friday. Fasting means no eating between meals with only one regular meal and two slight meals that don't add up to a regular

meal. Abstinence means no meat may be eaten on Ash Wednesday or any Friday of Lent by Catholics age 14-59. A Catholic has a serious obligation to obey these laws substantially, i.e., for the most part.

3. Attend Easter Triduim Liturgies if you can on Holy Thursday, Good Friday, and Easter Vigil.
4. Pray the Divine Mercy Novena in preparation for Divine Mercy Sunday (see prayer section).
5. Renew Baptismal promises at Easter.
6. Fulfill Divine Mercy Sunday Indulgence
7. Renew your consecration to Mary
8. Vote pro-life.
9. Make a retreat.

Part IX
Prayers

The Rosary

At Fatima, Mary told us to "Pray the Rosary everyday." As true children of Mary this is something that we should do.

Hail, Holy Queen

Hail, holy Queen, Mother of mercy; hail our life, our sweetness and our hope. To you we cry, poor banished children of Eve. To you do we send up our sighs, mourning and weeping in this valley of tears. Turn then, most gracious Advocate, your eyes and mercy towards us. And after this our exile shows unto us the blessed fruit of your womb, Jesus. O clement, O loving, O sweet Virgin Mary. Pray for us, O Holy Mother of God; that we may be made worthy of the promises of Christ.

Rosary Prayer

O God, whose only-begotten Son, by His life, death and resurrection, has purchased for us the rewards of eternal life; grant, we beseech You, that meditating upon these mysteries of the most holy rosary of the Blessed Virgin Mary, we may learn to imitate what they contain and obtain what they promise, through the same Christ our Lord. Amen.

The Fifteen Promises of Mary to Christians Who Recite the Rosary

1. Whoever shall faithfully serve me by the recitation of the rosary, shall receive signal graces.

2. I promise my special protection and the greatest graces to all those who shall recite the rosary.

3. The rosary shall be a powerful armor against hell, it will destroy vice, decrease sin, and defeat heresies.

4. It will cause virtue and good works to flourish; it will withdraw the hearts of men from the love of the world and its vanities, and will lift them to the desire of eternal things. Oh, that souls would sanctify themselves by this means.

5. The soul which recommends itself to me by the recitation of the rosary, shall not perish.

6. Whoever shall recite the rosary devoutly, applying himself to the consideration of its sacred mysteries shall never be conquered by misfortune. God will not chastise him in His justice, he shall not perish by an un-provided death; if he be just he shall remain in the grace of God, and become worthy of eternal life.

7. Whoever shall have a true devotion for the rosary shall not die without the sacraments of the Church.

8. Those who are faithful to recite the rosary shall have during their life and at their death the light of God and the plentitude of His graces; at the moment of

death they shall participate in the merits of the saints in paradise.

9. I shall deliver from purgatory those who have been devoted to the rosary.

10. The faithful children of the rosary shall merit a high degree of glory in heaven.

11. You shall obtain all you ask of me by the recitation of the rosary.

12. All those who propagate the holy rosary shall be aided by me in their necessities.

13. I have obtained from my Divine Son that all the advocates of the rosary shall have for intercessors the entire celestial court during their life and at the hour of death.

14. All who recite the rosary are my sons, and brothers of my only Son Jesus Christ.

15. Devotion to my rosary is a great sign of predestination.

The Memorare

Remember, O most gracious Virgin Mary that never was it known that anyone who fled to your protection, implored your help or sought your intercession, was left unaided. Inspired by this confidence, I fly to you, O Virgin of Virgins, my mother. To you do I come; before you I stand, sinful and sorrowful. O Mother of the Word Incarnate, despise not my petitions, but in your mercy, hear and answer me. Amen.

Marian Consecration and Scapular

Every Catholic should have a healthy devotion to Mary, the Mother of God and our mother. As he was dying, Jesus entrusted His mother into the care of the faithful disciple, John. The Gospel tells us that John took her into his home and we too, as faithful disciples, should take Mary into our hearts and allow her to be our mother.

Our relationship to Mary should mirror that of a faithful child towards his loving mother. After a period of spiritual preparation, every Catholic should make an act of consecration of himself to Mary. Essentially, this means to dedicate one's life to love and honor Mary, just as Jesus loved and honored her. It also means that we place ourselves under her protection and ask her intercession in everything. It is most appropriate to make this act of consecration on a Marian Feast Day and to renew it each year on that day.

After the act of consecration has been made, a person should wear the brown scapular everyday as an outward sign of your inner devotion to Mary. The scapular can be considered your "Marian Habit" or "uniform" which constantly reminds you of your relationship with Mary.

I love to wear the scapular and I will never give it up. It has brought tremendous help to me and I also treasure the promise that Mary gave to those who wear it with devotion, "Whoever dies wearing this scapular shall not suffer eternal fire."

Act of Consecration to Mary

Most holy Virgin Mary, Mother of God, I, N., although most unworthy to be thy servant, yet moved by thy wonderful compassion, and by my desire to serve thee, now choose thee, in presence of my guardian angel and of the whole celestial court, for my especial Lady, Advocate, and Mother: and I firmly purpose always to love and serve thee for the future, and to do whatever I can to induce others to love and serve thee also. I beseech thee, O Mother of God, by the blood which thy Son shed for me, to receive me into the number of thy servants, to be thy child and servant forever. Assist me in all my thoughts, words, and actions in every moment of my life, so that every step that I take, and every breath that I draw, may be directed to the greater glory of my God; and through thy most powerful intercession, may I never more offend my beloved Jesus, but may I glorify him, and love him in this life, and love thee, my most beloved and dear Mother, and thus love thee and enjoy thee in Heaven for all eternity, Amen.

My Mother Mary, I recommend my soul to thee, and especially at the hour of my death.

Act of Consecration to the Sacred Heart of Jesus

To the Sacred Heart of our Lord, Jesus Christ, I give myself and I consecrate my person and my life, my actions, pains, and sufferings, so that I may be unwilling to make use of any part of my being other than to honor, love, and glorify the Sacred Heart.

This is my unchanging purpose, namely, to be all His and to do all things for the love of Him, at the same time renouncing with all my heart whatever is displeasing to Him. I therefore take you, O Sacred Heart, to be the only object of my love, the guardian of my life, my assurance of salvation, the remedy of my weakness and inconstancy, the atonement for all the faults of my life, and my sure refuge at the hour of death.

Be then, O Heart of goodness, my justification before God the Father, and turn away from me the strokes of His righteous anger. O Heart of Love, I put all my confidence in You, for I fear everything from my own wickedness and frailty, but I hope for all things from Your goodness and bounty.

Remove from me all that can displease You or resist Your holy will; let Your pure love imprint Your image so deeply upon my heart that I shall never be able to forget You or to be separated from You.

May I obtain from Your loving kindness the grace of having my name written in Your heart, for in You I desire to place all my happiness and glory, living and dying in bondage to You.

The Twelve Promises of the Sacred Heart to St. Margaret Mary

1. I will give them all the graces necessary for their state in life.
2. I will give peace in their families.
3. I will console them in all their troubles.
4. They shall find in My Heart an assured refuge during life and especially at the hour of death.
5. I will pour abundant blessings upon all their undertakings.
6. Sinners shall find in My Heart the source and the infinite ocean of mercy.
7. Tepid souls shall become fervent.
8. Fervent souls shall speedily rise to great perfection.
9. I will bless the homes in which My Sacred Heart shall be exposed and honored.
10. I will give to priests the power to touch the most hardened hearts.
11. Those who propagate this devotion shall have their name written in My Heart, and it shall never be effaced.
12. The all-powerful love of My Heart will grant to all those who shall receive Communion on the First Friday of nine consecutive months the grace of final repentance; they shall not die under My displeasure, nor without receiving their Sacraments; My Heart shall be their assured refuge at that last hour.

Daily Prayer to the Sacred Heart of Jesus

Sacred Heart of Jesus today I wish to live in You, in Your grace, in which I desire at all costs to persevere. Keep me from sin and strengthen my will by helping me to keep watch over my senses, my imagination, and my heart. Help me to correct my faults, which are the source of sin. I beg you to do this, O Jesus, thorough Mary, Your Immaculate Mother.

Prayer to Christ the King

O Jesus Christ, I acknowledge thee as universal King. All that has been made, has been created for Thee. Exercise over me all Thy rights. I renew my baptismal vows, I renounce Satan, his pomps and his works; and I promise to live as a good Christian. Especially do I pledge myself to labor, to the best of my ability, for the triumph of the rights of God and Thy Church. Divine Heart of Jesus, to Thee do I proffer my poor services, laboring that all hearts may acknowledge Thy Sacred Kingship, and that thus the reign of Thy peace be established throughout the whole world. Amen.

Prayers of the Chaplet of the Divine Mercy

1. **The Sign of the Cross:** In the name of the Father, and the Son, and of the Holy Spirit. Amen.
2. **Opening Prayer (optional):** You expired, Jesus, but the source of life gushed forth for souls, and the ocean of mercy opened up for the whole world. O Fount of Life, unfathomable Divine Mercy, envelop the whole world and empty Yourself out upon us.

O Blood and Water, which gushed forth from the Heart of Jesus as a fount of mercy for us, I trust in You! (three times).

3. **The Our Father:** Our Father, who art in heaven hallowed by Thy name; Thy kingdom come; Thy will be done on earth as it is in heaven. Give us this day our daily bread; and forgive us our trespasses as we forgive those who trespass against us; and lead us not into temptation, but deliver us from evil. Amen.

4. **The Hail Mary:** Hail Mary, full of grace. The Lord is with you. Blessed are you among women, and blessed is the fruit of your womb, Jesus. Holy Mary, Mother of God, pray for us sinners, now and at the hour of our death. Amen.

5. **The Apostles' Creed:** I believe in God, the Father almighty, Creator of heaven and earth. I believe in Jesus Christ, His only Son, our Lord. He was conceived by the power of the Holy Spirit, and born of the Virgin Mary. He suffered under Pontius Pilate, was crucified, died, and was buried. He descended to the dead. On the third day He rose again. He ascended into heaven, and is seated at the right hand of the Father. He will come again to judge the living and the dead. I believe in the Holy Spirit, the Holy Catholic Church, the communion of saints, the forgiveness of sins, the resurrection of the body, and the life everlasting. Amen.

6. **On the "Our Father" bead before each decade:** Eternal Father, I offer You the Body and Blood, Soul and Divinity of Your dearly beloved Son, Our Lord

Jesus Christ, in atonement for our sins and those of the whole world.

7. **On the "Hail Mary" beads of each decade:** For the sake of His sorrowful Passion, have mercy on us and on the whole world.

8. **Repeat: "Eternal Father"** and **"For the Sake of His sorrowful Passion"** (Number 6 & 7) prayers for four more decades.

9. **After 5 decades, the concluding doxology** (three times): Holy God, Holy Mighty One, Holy Immortal One, have mercy on us and on the whole world.

10. **Closing Prayer (optional):** Eternal God, in whom mercy is endless, and the treasury of compassion inexhaustible, look kindly upon us, and increase Your mercy in us, that in difficult moments, we might not despair, nor become despondent, but with great confidence, submit ourselves to Your holy will, which is Love and Mercy Itself. Amen.

The Seven Offerings of the Precious Blood of Jesus

Eternal Father, we offer you the Precious Blood of Jesus, poured out on the cross and offered daily on the altar, for the glory of your name, for the coming of your kingdom, and for the salvation of all people. Glory be to the Father... As it was in the beginning... Praise and thanksgiving be evermore to Jesus, who with his Blood has saved us.

Eternal Father, we offer you the Precious Blood of Jesus, poured out on the cross and offered daily on the altar, for the spread of the Church, for Pope Benedict XVI, for Bishops, priests, and religious, and for the sanctification of all the people of God. Glory be to the Father... Praise and...

Eternal Father, we offer you the Precious Blood of Jesus, poured out on the cross and offered daily on the altar, for the conversion of sinners, for the loving acceptance of your word, and for the union of all Christians. Glory be to the Father... Praise and...

Eternal Father, we offer you the Precious Blood of Jesus, poured out on the cross and offered daily on the altar, for our civil authorities, for the strengthening of public morals, and for peace and justice among all nations. Glory be to the Father... Praise and...

Eternal Father, we offer you the Precious Blood of Jesus, poured out on the cross and offered daily on the altar, for the sanctification of our work and our suffering, for the poor and the rich, the sick and the afflicted, and for all who rely on our prayers. Glory be to the Father... Praise and...

Eternal Father, we offer you the Precious Blood of Jesus, poured out on the cross and offered daily on the altar, for our own special needs, both spiritual and temporal, for those of our relatives, friends and benefactors, and also for those of our enemies. Glory be to the Father... Praise and...

Eternal Father, we offer you the Precious Blood of Jesus, poured out on the cross and offered daily on the altar, for those who are to die this day, for the souls in purgatory, and for our own final union with Christ in glory. Glory be to the Father... Praise and... Glory to the Blood of Jesus. Now and forever. Amen.

Morning Offering

O Jesus, through that Immaculate Heart of Mary, I offer You my prayers, works, joys, and sufferings of this day in union with the Holy Sacrifice of the Mass throughout the world. I offer them for all the intentions of Your Sacred Heart: the salvation of souls, reparation for sin, and the reunion of all Christians. I offer them for the intentions of our Bishops and of all our associates, and in particular for those recommended by our Holy Father this month.

Travel Prayer

(Pray This Every Time You Drive)

Dear Jesus, please protect us on the highway. Don't let us hurt anyone and don't let anyone hurt us. Help us to bring your love to everyone we meet.

Act of Contrition

O my God, I am heartily sorry for having offended You, and I detest all my sins, because of Thy just punishments, but most of all because they have offended thee, my God, who are all good and deserving of all my love. I firmly resolve, with the help of Thy grace, to sin no more and to avoid the near occasion of sin. Amen.

Pardon Prayer

O my God, I believe, I adore, I hope and I love Thee! And I ask pardon for those who do not believe, do not adore, do not hope, and do not love Thee.

Prayer to St. Michael

St. Michael the Archangel, defend us in Battle; be our protection against the wickedness and snares of the Devil. May God rebuke him we humbly pray, and do Thou, O Prince of the Heavenly Host, by the power of God, thrust into Hell Satan and all other evil spirits, who prowl throughout the world, seeking the ruin of souls. Amen.

Prayer before a Crucifix

Behold, my beloved and good Jesus, I cast myself upon my knees in your sight, and with the most fervent desire of my soul I pray and beseech You to impress upon my heart lively sentiments of faith, hope, and charity, with true repentance for my sins and a most firm desire of amendment; while with deep affection and grief of soul I consider within myself and mentally contemplate your five most precious wounds, having before my eyes that which David the prophet long ago spoke about You, my Jesus: "They have pierced my hands and my feet; I can count all my bones."

Act of Consecration to the Holy Spirit

On my knees before the great multitude of heavenly witnesses, I offer myself, soul and body to You, Eternal

Spirit of God. I adore the brightness of Your purity, the unerring keenness of Your justice, and the might of Your love. You are the Strength and Light of my soul. In You I live and move and am. I desire never to grieve You by unfaithfulness to grace and I pray with all my heart to be kept from the smallest sin against You. Mercifully guard my every thought and grant that I may always watch for Your light, and listen to Your voice, and follow Your gracious inspirations. I cling to You and give myself to You and ask You, by Your compassion to watch over me in my weakness. Holding the pierced Feet of Jesus and looking at His Five Wounds, and trusting in His Precious Blood and adoring His opened Side and stricken Heart, I implore You, Adorable Spirit, Helper of my infirmity, to keep me in Your grace that I may never sin against You. Give me grace, O Holy Spirit, Spirit of the Father and the Son to stay with You always and everywhere.

Examination of Conscience

1. **I am the Lord your God. You shall not have strange gods before me.**

   Do I give God time everyday in prayer? Do I seek to love Him with my whole heart? Have I been involved with superstitious practices or have I been involved with the occult? Have I ever received Communion in the state of mortal sin? Have I deliberately told a lie in Confession or have I withheld a mortal sin from the priest in Confession?

2. **You shall not take the name of the Lord your God in vain.**

   Have I used God's name in vain, lightly, or carelessly? Have I been angry with God? Have I wished evil upon any other person? Have I insulted a sacred person or abused a sacred object?

3. **Remember to keep holy the Lord's Day.**

   Have I deliberately missed Mass on Sundays or Holy Days of Obligation? Have I tried to observe Sunday as a family day and a day of rest? Do I do needless work on Sunday?

4. **Honor your father and mother.**

   Do I honor and obey my parents? Do I try to bring peace into my home life? Do I care for my aged and infirm relatives? Do I give proper respect to legitimate authorities?

5. **You shall not kill.**

   Have I had an abortion or encouraged anyone to have an abortion? Have I physically harmed anyone? Have I abused alcohol or drugs? Did I give scandal to anyone, thereby leading him or her into sin? Have I been angry or resentful? Have I harbored hatred in my heart?

6. **You shall not commit adultery.**

   Have I engaged in any sexual activity outside of marriage? Have I used any methods of contraception or artificial birth control? Have I been guilty of masturbation? Have I respected all members of the opposite sex, or have I thought of people as objects? Have I been guilty of any homosexual activity? Do I seek to be chaste in my thoughts, words, and actions? Am I careful to dress modestly?

7. **You shall not steal.**

   Have I stolen what is not mine? Have I returned or made restitution for what I have stolen? Do I waste time at work, school, or at home? Do I gamble excessively, thereby denying my family of their needs? Do I pay my debts promptly? Do I seek to share what I have with the poor? Have I been honest and fair in all of my business dealings? Have I paid the taxes that I owe?

8. **You shall not bear false witness against your neighbor.**

   Have I lied? Have I gossiped? Am I sincere in my dealing with others? Am I critical, negative, or uncharitable in my thoughts of others? Do I keep secret what should be kept confidential?

9. **You shall not desire your neighbor's wife.**

   Have I consented to impure thoughts? Have I caused them by impure reading, movies, conversation, or curiosity? Do I seek to control my imagination? Do I pray at once to banish impure thoughts or temptations?

10. **You shall not desire your neighbor's goods.**

    Am I jealous of what other people have? Do I envy other people's families or possessions? Am I greedy or selfish? Are material possessions the purpose of my life? Do I trust that God will care for all of my material and spiritual needs?

I would be delighted to speak to your group or parish. Normally, I do not charge a speaking fee. To schedule an appearance please call (937) 295-2626.

To purchase additional copies of this book please use the following pricing information.

Number of Copies	Price per Copy
1	$11.99
2-19	$10.99
20+	$9.99

These prices include tax, shipping, and handling in the United States.

Mail your payment to:
Henry Cordonnier
1771 Russia-Houston Rd.
Russia, Ohio 45363
or call
(937) 295-2626
or visit
www.mygospelbook.com